MICROCOSM · PUBLISHING

MICROCOSM PUBLISHING is Portland's most diversified publishing house and distributor, with a focus on the colorful, authentic, and empowering. Our books and zines have put your power in your hands since 1996, equipping readers to make positive changes in their lives and in the world around them. Microcosm emphasizes skill-building, showing hidden histories, and fostering creativity through challenging conventional publishing wisdom with books and bookettes about DIY skills, food, bicycling, gender, self-care, and social justice. What was once a distro and record label started by Joe Biel in a drafty bedroom was determined to be *Publishers Weekly*'s fastest-growing publisher of 2022 and #3 in 2023 and 2024, and is now among the oldest independent publishing houses in Portland, OR, and Cleveland, OH. We are a politically moderate, centrist publisher in a world that has inched to the right for the past 80 years.

WELCOME!

So you want to organize a conference? This zine will offer practical tips, templates, and guidance for organizing a conference from a queer, feminist, and social justice–oriented perspective. No matter the kind of conference you are interested in organizing, whether large or small, online, in-person, hybrid, synchronous, or asynchronous, this zine includes what you need to know from the smallest details—such as what to have in your bag on the day(s) of the conference—to large topics—such as choosing a location, selecting presenters, funding, designing conference materials, working with community partners, and so much more!

How we do the work is the work. Drawing on my experience organizing several conferences including the Queer Food Conference; the Food, Feminism, and Fermentation Conference; the Food, Feminism, and Technology Conference; 6+ Feminist Research Colloquiums; and more than 100 events for the Disrupting Disruptions: Feminist and Accessible Publishing, Communications, and Tech Speaker and Workshop Series, with this zine, I hope to help you organize a conference that reflects the ethos that inspired your conference in the first place. We will explore how decisions over signage, website design, food, pricing, location, technology, and so much more can foreground queer, feminist, accessible, and social justice-oriented inclusive principles. This zine will help you host a conference in which everyone who takes part feels included, supported, and valued!

How to Use This Zine

Feel welcome to use this zine in any order. You can flip to different sections as they are most useful for you. Some sections include templates to adapt for your needs. The final pages of the zine include worksheets for helping you organize your own conference.

While I may mention certain applications and software, technology is ever-evolving. I encourage you to focus more on the technological capabilities of any tool (whether paper, email, computer software, or a phone app) and how they can serve the values of your conference rather than the exact software I discuss.

This zine contains information that will help guide your decisions to ensure that your conference is inclusive and reflects your goals and values.

TYPES OF CONFERENCES

In the most basic sense, conferences are about bringing people together. There are several types of conferences: workshops, colloquiums, conference-conferences, conventions, alternative conferences, and unconferences. The main differences between conference types are the size and duration.

Terminology varies by region, field, and individual preference, but there are some general differences.

Typically, **workshops** consist of a small group of people ranging from 5 to 30 participants focused on a specific goal. Workshops can be short or last several days. For example, a seed saving workshop would include workshop leaders who would share information about the topic and participants who could experiment with hands-on methods with a community of learners. Leaders might rotate throughout the day, with different participants leading mini-workshops within the larger workshop about specific topics.

Colloquiums can be upwards of 50 participants and often consist of several panels or events around a related topic. The annual Feminist Research Colloquium I organize in Montréal creates a space for undergraduate and graduate students to share their ongoing research on gender, sexuality, feminist, and social justice studies with their peers, professors, friends, and larger community. Some folks would also call this a symposium—like I said, terms are flexible.

Conferences are often even larger and may welcome 40 to over 2000 people, gathering around either a related topic or a shared field or discipline. Conference-conferences center knowledge exchange, foster professional development, and disseminate findings or practices. For 2 days, the Food, Feminism, and Fermentation Conference brought together scholars, journalists, artists, activists, farmers, chefs, cooks, baristas, brewers, authors, sommeliers, industry professionals, and curators all interested in the topic of feminist fermentation. The conference-conference format enables the sharing of information, networking, and socializing.

Conventions are events organized around a specific industry, interest group, or fandom that provide a platform for enthusiasts to connect. Conventions tend to be larger events, with a greater emphasis on material or economic exchange. Zine conventions, small press conventions, and comic conventions often include presentations. Many conventions include a space where participants can have a table where they can exchange and/or sell their own publications and chat with other enthusiasts.

Alternative conferences experiment with format, timing, and how people can participate. The DIY Methods Conference is a mostly screen-free, remote participation conference where attendees submit zines on their topics by a certain date to the conference organizers, who then distribute the zines via mail and online.

Unconferences are participant-oriented meetings where, usually during the event, attendees decide on the agenda, discussion topics, workshops, and even sometimes the time and venues. Any participant who wants to initiate a discussion on a topic can claim a time and a space in the unconference schedule. Other sessions are for open discussion. The idea behind unconferences is to focus on conversation over presentation. Unconferences, which tend to be smaller events, often are most fruitful when participants already have a high level of expertise or knowledge related to the conference's topic. For an unconference to be effective, there still needs to be a framework within which the experimentation can happen. While the scheduling of exact panels and discussions might happen on the day of the event, having a venue with accessible rooms, assistive technologies, and refreshments remains important. Organizers of unconferences can still make use of this zine while developing the unconference infrastructure.

Remember, none of these definitions are hard and fast, but rather give a sense of the possibilities of scale. Workshops, colloquiums, conferences, conventions, and unconferences can occur in-person, virtually, or in hybrid format. We'll discuss format more in the pages to come, but first, let's look at a typical timeline for organizing a conference.

TIMELINE FOR ORGANIZING A CONFERENCE

While conferences can be organized in a shorter amount of time, below is a one-year timeline. I prefer to provide a less compacted schedule so that you feel like you can have fun planning the conference and you can mitigate some of the stress that can come with conference organizing. The larger and more complicated the conference, the longer you will need to plan it.

Having a longer timeline does not only benefit you as a conference organizer. Sharing information in advance also provides time to people who might need to travel from out of town to attend, allowing them to figure out their travel plans, arrange child or elder care, plan time off from work, and/or make other arrangements.

As you organize your specific conference, you will be able to adapt this timeline to your specific needs.

One Year (or More) Out

- ☐ Start to daydream: What do you want your conference to look like? What are the themes? Dream big!
- ☐ Begin to brainstorm practical details: See Worksheet #1 at the back of the zine for directed brainstorming techniques.
- ☐ Look at what grants are available. What kinds of funding sources might you access? Grants are often on yearly or biyearly schedules, so make sure you find out deadlines far in advance. See if your town, city, or community has any grants or funds available to provide at least partial support.
- ☐ Begin to brainstorm potential sponsors.
- ☐ Determine whether the event will be hybrid, in-person, or virtual.
- ☐ Determine what type of conference the event will be (workshop, colloquium, conference-conference, convention, alternative conference, or unconference).
- ☐ Figure out if you have any start-up funds available. You might need funds to put a deposit on a venue or other rentals.

11 to 12 Months Out

- ☐ Figure out the venue/location. Book it as soon as you can.
- ☐ Figure out your dates.
- ☐ Determine if you need to apply for any kinds of permits or licenses.
- ☐ If you haven't started to apply for grants and want to, get on it!

11 Months Out

- ☐ Start to create a conference website with basic information on it, such as conference name, location, date, and a note about when more information will be forthcoming (more information on website design is in this zine!)
- ☐ Craft your CFP (Call for Papers/ Presentations/Panels/Workshops/Roundtables/Events/Performances/Etc).
- ☐ Design your form for presenter applications.
- ☐ Determine how you will decide which presenters are accepted and rejected.
- ☐ Determine if there will be a committee to go through the presenter applications (and then make the committee).

10 Months Out

- ☐ It is useful to have a rough sense of your budget and what conference fees will be at this point so you can share fee information with presenter applicants.
- ☐ Release your Call for Papers (CFP) and Presenter Application Form at the same time (the link to the Presenter Application Form should be included in the CFP). Make sure that these materials are available on your conference website.
- ☐ Begin advertising the CFP and your early conference website at this point. It is okay that you will have pages of the website that state "details to come." Share the CFP and website URL on listservs, social media, and even via flyers or posters if you mostly plan to involve folks who live locally.
- ☐ If you plan to have a conference keynote speaker or speakers, contact them now. Make sure to include information about any honorariums (cash) you may provide for their talk and if you are going to pay for their travel. Share your expectations about the length and format of the presentation.

9 Months Out

- ☐ Continue to advertise the CFP and conference website.
- ☐ You might be able to work with journalists to help get the word out! At the very least, you can start to build relationships with journalists now if press coverage of the event is useful.
- ☐ Are you interested in collaborating with other organizations or individuals to have conference-adjacent events? For example, maybe you will provide programming from 9:00 to 5:00 each day of the conference, but to encourage participants to visit other parts of the area or support local businesses in the city, you might have dinners, parties, dances, or even town tours held after 5:00. Start to make these arrangements.

8 Months Out

- ☐ Presenter applications are due. I usually give a 48-hour grace period for late applications, but you might decide to have a hard cut-off. If you do not receive enough applications, you can always extend the deadline.
- ☐ Begin to read through presenter applications and rank the applications. The larger the conference, the longer reading through ap-

plications will take. You might consider doing this work within a committee.

☐ Decide what software you will use for conference registration. If you are charging for registration, you will need to pick a strategy for collecting fees and tracking payment. Depending on the needs of your conference partners, you may want to include conference-adjacent events on the main registration form, as "add-ons," or have separate ticketing links for these events.

6 to 7 Months Out

☐ Let presenter applicants know whether or not they were accepted, wait-listed, or rejected.

☐ Provide accepted presenters with a link to register for the conference first, especially if you have limited space capacity. Explain that the presenter must register by a certain date to confirm their participation.

☐ If you have a waitlist, start to pull folks from the waitlist if people decline their presenter offers.

5 to 6 Months Out

☐ Create the tentative presentation schedule. Put this schedule along with abstracts on the conference website.

☐ Write the announcement for conference registration. A few sentences describing the who, what, where, why, and how to register for the conference is key. You might create a visual component to accompany the announcement.

☐ Open registration for non-presenter participants.

☐ If you are hiring caterers, book them now!

☐ Start to connect with journalists and media folks who might want to participate. It is typical to provide press passes.

☐ Update the conference website with information about accessibility, other things to do nearby, and where participants can stay if they are traveling from out-of-town.

4 to 6 Months Out

☐ Create the conference program/booklet.

☐ Update the conference website with any new information.

☐ If you are distributing conference SWAG (souvenirs, wearables, and gifts), start to design it and order it. If there are items that will be for sale, you can also have a pre-order form or order link on your website.

- ☐ Monitor conference registrations. You might have to publicize the conference more or offer incentives for early registration. Or if spots are filling up quickly, share that information on listservs and social media.
- ☐ Set up meetings with potential vendors. Find out what they need, such as electricity, tables, space, etc.
- ☐ If there will be a bookseller interested in selling books written by conference presenters, connect authors with the bookseller.

2 to 3 Months Out

- ☐ Form your conference crew/volunteer team.
- ☐ Design and order conference t-shirts, hats, or uniforms for the conference crew/volunteer team. These items can help participants identify the crew during the event.
- ☐ Ask presenters on roundtables, panels, and/or group presentations to plan to have slideshows or presentations within a single file or link—or even a single computer—to reduce tech friction during the event.
- ☐ If speaker bios will be read and were not previously collected, make sure to connect presenters with the person reading the bios so they can be gathered in advance.
- ☐ Continue to publicize the conference.

1 to 2 Months Out

- ☐ Print your conference booklet (if having printed programs/booklets).
- ☐ Continue to publicize the conference.
- ☐ You will likely receive lots of questions from presenters and attendees via email. In addition to responding to individual emails, update the conference website with information that might be of use for other participants.
- ☐ Follow up with your participants, vendors, and volunteers to make sure everyone is feeling set. It's useful to check in with folks.
- ☐ You will likely have some folks drop out and have to move some bits of the schedule around. This is normal.

Week Before the Conference

- ☐ Confirm details with your conference crew.
- ☐ Confirm details with the venue.
- ☐ Confirm final details with the caterers, including where to park.
- ☐ Send a reminder email to all participants with important conference details (see the template on page 45).
- ☐ Create directional signs to set up at the venue to guide people to conference locations, including all-gender washrooms.
- ☐ If your conference is virtual or hybrid and presenters have special panelist links, make sure they have their links.

Day Before the Conference

- ☐ Have a run-through meeting with your conference crew/volunteer team.
- ☐ Set up all materials, tables, and tech that you can set up in advance.
- ☐ If you are able to have vendors' materials in a locked room, you can have vendors bring their materials the day before the conference so they don't have to arrive early.
- ☐ Send a reminder email to all participants with important conference details.
- ☐ If you are hosting a hybrid or virtual conference, send out the virtual meeting, virtual webinar, or livestream links.
- ☐ Confirm final details with the caterer for Day 1 of the conference.
- ☐ Send the reminder email to your conference crew/volunteer team, including the shift schedule.
- ☐ Print out the crew schedule, print off your day-of checklist, print conference schedules, print signs for the venue. Print off a list of your crew members' phone numbers in case you need to reach them. Print off a list of emergency contact numbers. Put these materials in your conference bag.
- ☐ If virtual or hybrid and presenters have special panelist links, re-email them their links. Make it easy for people to find their links!
- ☐ You will also likely receive lots of last minute questions via email. Be on top of your email today.
- ☐ Pack your bag for the next morning (see: what to have in your bag on page 63)

- ☐ Try to get a good night's sleep!

Day 1 of the Conference

- ☐ Send an early morning reminder email for participants.
- ☐ Arrive early. Try to arrive at least 90 minutes before the first participants arrive.
- ☐ Have your day of checklist with the important micro details you will need to remember during the event.
- ☐ Make sure that the sign-in/registration table has all of the required materials. (More information in this zine on page 58!)
- ☐ Be ready to greet the caterer and any vendors that arrive. Have conference crew members already allocated to help them set up.
- ☐ Make sure there is proper signage for the washrooms, including arrows pointing to the closest gender neutral washrooms. If there aren't already tampons and pads in the washrooms, put out a basket with some freely available.
- ☐ Check that all of the volunteers on the first shift have arrived.
- ☐ Make sure the tech is ready in each room. You might do this with your conference crew and IT team.
- ☐ Have your phone volume on in case the caterer, another vendor, or crew member calls.
- ☐ If you are making introductory remarks, start on time to set a precedent for being on time for the rest of the day.
- ☐ Have your device to check for last minute emails. Check throughout the day.
- ☐ Rove throughout the conference, being available to answer questions or concerns from your team or participants.
- ☐ If you are running a hybrid conference, in addition to the role of the room monitors, jump into the different web streams, virtual meetings, or virtual meetings throughout the meeting to just check that the experience is going well for virtual participants.
- ☐ While you might be able to attend an event or two, you will likely need to be on call throughout the event.
- ☐ Check in with the vendors to make sure their needs are being met.

- During the day, your role will be facilitating the conference. Make sure to network with conference participants, checking in on their needs and helping connect participants.
- Check with your conference crew that the bathrooms are clean and have enough toilet paper (have a crew member on top of this).
- If there is a midday break, it is a great time to check that the rooms are clean, the tech is running, and the vendors are happy.
- If there are journalists attending, make sure to connect them with different participants who can speak about the conference. Make sure the journalists are receiving the resources that they need.
- At the end of the day, participate in clean up. Even if you have a conference crew, clean up work is a shared effort!
- At the end of the day, touch base with your crew to see what went well and what could be improved for the next day/ subsequent days. See **Worksheet #2**.
- If there is an after hours event, attend at least part of it to be supportive of your conference partners. If you can't attend yourself, try to have your conference co-organizer or at least members of your crew attend.
- Backup your photos of the event (and if someone is responsible for taking photos, ask them to do so too).
- Consider sharing some visual representation of Day 1 of the conference on social media.
- Prep the email you will send to all conference participants for the next morning.
- If you just have one conference shirt/uniform, wash it for the next day.
- Repack your conference bag for the next day.
- Rest!

Day 2+ of the Conference

- Repeat most of the sequence from Day 1. However, you will have a better sense of the flow.
- You might be able to attend more events on Day 2 if the conference is flowing well.
- If there is an after hours celebration, try to attend.

Post Conference (1 to 3 days after)

- ☐ You did it! Take a moment to acknowledge this giant accomplishment!
- ☐ If you didn't finish cleaning up the evening of the last conference day, finish cleaning up.
- ☐ Send a thank you email/note to the conference crew/volunteers.
- ☐ Send a thank you email/note to the caterers. Make sure the caterer has received payment. If you need a receipt or invoice to get refunded from a grant or organization, make sure to collect it now.
- ☐ Send a thank you email/note to the vendors.
- ☐ Send a thank you email/note to conference partners.
- ☐ If you invited keynote speakers, performers, or other folks you need to pay an honorarium, make sure to send the honoraria ASAP. You might need to follow up with these folks about documents such as tax forms, routing numbers, and other details.
- ☐ If working with journalists, you will likely have follow up chats. Write them a thank you email.
- ☐ Make a list of what went well and what mistakes you made. These moments are learning opportunities. Write them down while they are still fresh in your mind.
- ☐ Collect photos from your conference crew and/or participants.
- ☐ Share images from the conference on your conference social media, website, and with participants.
- ☐ Rest!

Post Conference (further out)

- ☐ Getting ready for the next one? Do you want to host another edition? Do you want to help someone else host another one? If you are hosting a yearly conference, you might start the cycle again quite soon after the end of this one.
- ☐ Publications? Some conferences lead to anthologies, collaborations, and a variety of publications. If you haven't already started to work on one, it is best to start working on it while the conference is still fresh in peoples' minds.
- ☐ If it is the first conference of its kind, how will you help folks stay in touch? Will you share email addresses? Create a directory? A listserv? Something else?

Every conference is unique, but this timeline provides a general sense of the tasks involved. The size of the conference will greatly impact your task list.

SIZE

Conferences can range widely in size. The scale of your conference will impact all subsequent decisions. Finding a venue for 20 people is very different from finding a venue for 200 or 2000 people. Providing food and SWAG for 50 people is a different undertaking than for 5000. Your decisions over size will greatly impact later choices about venue, format, cost, applications for presenters, and collaborators.

Several factors can help you decide the size of your conference, including location, topic of the conference (how niche is your topic?), the amount of time you can dedicate to organizing the conference, and budget. If your conference is for an organization that has 70 members that all would need to attend, then you already know your general size. If you need or want to host your conference at a specific location that has an occupancy capacity of 50 people, then the decision is made for you (though you can likely accept 5 to 8% more people than the capacity due to last minute cancellations and not everyone attending every event). However, physical space is not the only mitigating factor if you have virtual or hybrid components.

If this is your first time organizing a conference, consider starting with a smaller event of 50 people or fewer. The larger the conference, the more components you will have to manage. You can always organize a larger conference in the future.

LOCATION

There are many factors to consider when determining the location for your conference. Will your conference be in-person only? Virtual only? Hybrid? Your choices around location will impact who the conference is accessible for. In-person conferences mean that either people have to live locally or travel, which may not be financially accessible for everyone. People who are unable to leave their home due to caregiving responsibilities or different disabilities will not be able to participate. Virtual conferences require access to a strong internet connection, a technological device, and often a quiet, private space for participation. Hybrid conferences can expand participation, mitigating some of the barriers of virtual or in-person only conferences, but are more difficult to organize and not every event translates into hybrid format well.

General Location Factors to Consider for In-Person Events (or the In-Person Components of Hybrid Events)

When it comes to booking physical spaces or venues for your conference, there are a lot of things to consider if you want your event to be inclusive. Cost of renting or using a space can impact whether or not you charge for the event and this in turn can impact who can attend. The availability of the space may affect the date/timing of the event. If you decide to have an event outdoors, you might have to take rental costs of port-o-potties, electrical connections, and table rentals into consideration. The structure of the space can also impact accessibility and the kinds of programming you can offer.

Below are suggestions to consider when choosing a space for your event.

- Can the room only be entered by climbing stairs or a steep hill? Stairs mean that people with reduced mobility and wheelchair users will not be able to attend. If there are elevators, are they wide enough for wheelchairs and scooters?
- Are the door frames of the venue wide enough for a wheelchair or scooter to pass through? 32 inches or 82 cm (preferably wider)? Is there a bump over the threshold? Even a 1 inch or 2.5 cm bump can pose an issue for wheelchair users. Threshold ramps can mitigate this problem.
- Have you allocated space for service animals? Is there access to the outdoors for service dogs?
- If doors are closed, do the doors have lever handles and/or are they equipped with an automatic opener? If not, will you have someone at the entrance to welcome people into the room?
- Is there a public transit option for people to travel to the event? Public transport is a class and environmental issue. (If you're in a major metropolitan area, Google added wheelchair accessible routes to Google Maps on both desktop and mobile.)
- Are there designated parking spots near the entrance for people with disabilities?
- Is there a barrier-free path for people to travel from the parking lot or drop-off area to the venue entrance?
- If you are hosting the event in a place with snow or ice, will the paths be cleared?
- If the event is being held at an outdoor site, will the surface be accessible for persons using wheelchairs and scooters?
- If the main entrance is not accessible, is there a sign clearly visible at the front of the building that indicates the location of an accessible entrance? Make sure to circulate information about accessibil-

ity features in advance of the event as well. (The conference website is a great place for this information).

- Is there a wheelchair accessible washroom/bathroom? Are the sinks reachable from a wheelchair?
- Is there an all-gender washroom/bathroom? If the venue does not have a single-use washroom or all-gender washrooms, are you able to temporarily change the bathroom signs for the event? The ability to access a washroom is a basic human right. A lack of all-gender washrooms can make your event non-inclusive for trans and non-binary individuals.
- Is there a space for people who are nursing? Is there an electrical outlet for breast/chest pumps?
- Will you be able to provide chairs for people who may need to sit? This can be particularly important for, but not limited to, people with various disabilities, the elderly, and pregnant individuals.
- Can you rearrange chairs so that wheelchair users can have a seat at the table? Near the stage? Is it possible to arrange sitting in circles, so that people who are hard of hearing can see people's faces?
- Will your conference take place in one room? Or multiple? How far is the distance between these spaces? Does your schedule have enough time to accommodate movement between these spaces?
- How will you ensure people with a low-stimuli threshold will be able to find a quieter space?
- Are you able to control the lighting? Fluorescent lighting can cause headaches, which make it difficult to participate.
- Can you guarantee a scent-free environment, including in the washrooms? Due to scent sensitivities, which can cause nausea and headaches, ask participants in advance to refrain from using strong perfumes and soaps.
- If hosting the conference outdoors, do you need to rent toilets? Do you have the electricity you need? What about rain? Will you rent a tent? Will you need to rent tables and chairs?
- If you are hosting a multi-day conference, is there lodging nearby? Are you able to offer lodging at a discounted cost or at a sliding scale?

It will also be important to consider your technological needs for the conference. While the tech section will discuss this more, some questions to consider are:

- Do rooms already have projectors? Can you rent or bring in your own projectors?
- What about sound systems? Microphones?

- Are there enough outlets? Does the venue charge extra for electricity use?
- Is there wifi? How can people access it? How will the network and password information be distributed?

Booking Rooms/Spaces/Venues/Locations

Your budget will also influence your choice of venue. When renting a venue, it is important to check on the following questions:

- What is the cost per hour? (Be sure to account for set up and take down times.)
- What equipment is provided and what do you have to provide (chairs, tables, sound equipment, etc.)?
- Are there limitations regarding what you can do in the venue? If you plan to provide food, do you have to use their in-house caterer? How much noise are you allowed to make? Do you have to hire security?
- Are you responsible for cleaning the space? The bathrooms?
- If there is no all-gender washroom/bathroom on site, can you change the signs for the day (even by putting a piece of paper over the permanent sign)?
- If you are in an outdoor space, do you need a permit?
- If you plan to serve alcohol, do you need a permit?
- If you do serve alcohol, is there space available for sober social hour events?

Free or Low-Cost Options

Using free or low-cost spaces is my preference as it means that the conference budget (which sometimes is zero dollars) is not eaten up by the space rental. Depending on the community you are trying to reach with your conference, these options may encourage or dissuade participation. Not everyone feels comfortable going to a university campus, a community center, or an event in a church basement, even though these may be low cost options.

Libraries

Libraries offer more than books (though books are wonderful)! Your local library may have a room for gatherings, may have maker-spaces, and more! Check out what kinds of resources are available. Even if the library isn't the right venue for your conference, you might be able to borrow audio/visual equipment or other necessary materials there.

University or College Campuses / Schools
If you are a student or faculty member, it is usually possible to rent spaces on campus for free or low cost (especially if you are part of a student group, club, or organization). If you aren't a student or faculty member, can you collaborate with a student or faculty member for your event to get access to this free space? From classrooms to concert halls, universities and colleges offer a wide variety of spaces. Booking through the events office of a university might lead to higher costs than working with individuals you might know at a university who can book spaces for free or low cost through their department. After graduating high school, I never held an event in a high school again, but elementary, middle, and high schools might be options for you too.

Community Centers
"Community center" is a broad term that can refer to a wide range of resources and spaces available. They are typically public or semi-public locations where members of a community tend to gather for group activities, social support, public information, and more. They may sometimes be open for use by the whole community or only for a specialized group within the greater community.

Religious Organizations
Some religious groups will rent out their spaces, particularly basements, even to non-community members. These spaces tend to be available at low or no cost. The choice to meet in the basement of a church, temple, or synagogue may deter participation from potential attendees, and potentially create obstacles to accessibility.

Local Music and Arts Venues
Depending on the venue, there can be a wide range of fees. Your city or town might have a cafe, restaurant, pub, bar, or gallery that offers free or low cost space or has sliding scales for events. Businesses that are explicit about their feminist, social justice, or anarchist politics tend to have more affordable options.

Public Parks
While public parks may have rules about the size of the gathering and time of day it can take place—and may require permits—many public parks have bathrooms, running water, and some kind of structure. Using these facilities can be free or low cost.

On the Land
Want to host an outdoor conference? You will likely need to also rent a tent for rain or to block direct sunlight. You might need to rent toilets and bring extension cords for electricity (or be off the grid), and don't forget: water! Maybe you will organize a solar powered outdoor hybrid conference—wonderful! Hosting an event outdoors is not necessarily cheaper than using an indoor venue due to rental costs.

Not Low Cost: Hotels and Conference/Convention Centers
Especially if you are hosting a conference with thousands of people, you might consider hosting your conference in a hotel or a conference/convention center. The benefit of hosting conferences in these spaces is that the facility is used to hosting these kinds of events. The downside is that the costs can be exorbitant and might mean you have to charge over 100 dollars per participant ticket. You might have to book these spaces more than 1 year in advance. Some hotels also offer packages which include discounted rooms.

It can be helpful to talk to other event organizers from your town or city to get local tips and tricks. Also if you are going to pay to use a space, it is great if your dollars can support a business or organization that you respect.

Choosing a Virtual Conference Format

Virtual conferences can enable people from around the world to connect synchronously or asynchronously (people can watch or listen after the recording). By going virtual, the financial and environmental cost of travel to in-person person conferences can be reduced. However, it is important to remember that virtual conferences still have a material impact through electricity, internet infrastructure, and the mining of materials for our computers and devices. While digital tools expand accessibility in some senses, it is important to note that marginalized communities are more likely to face online harassment, including trolling and doxxing. Security breaches during virtual conferences and events have resulted in "zoombombings"— a phenomenon in which people use the platform to harass the presenter or participants. Additionally, if the nature of your conference is particularly political, you will want to consider the cybersecurity of your event. Online spaces can be violent spaces.

Video Chat/Webinar Services
Video chat and webinar services can be useful for conference events in which you want the audience to be able to speak and ask questions. Some software allows you to record the video chat and share the footage after the conference.

During 2020 and the subsequent COVID-19 pandemic years, many folks became more familiar with video chat services such as Zoom, Google Meet, Microsoft Teams, and Skype. Jitsi is a free and open source video conferencing tool (Jitsi.org). Bluejeans is another option. For many of these services, use is free up to a specified number of users or for a certain amount of time. Services such as Zoom also provide webinar options, which allow a greater control over security features. If you are running multiple events simultaneously during your conference, you will need to enable several meetings or webinars at once and make all of these links available to the conference participants so they can pop into the room or webinar of their choice.

Features on these platforms continue to change. You can often enable features for language interpretation including sign language and CART captioning. If you are not working with a human CART captioner, make sure to enable auto-captions on the platform you use if they are not already enabled in order to increase accessibility. Captions can be useful for people who are Deaf, hard of hearing, are participating in a second language, and more!

If you are sharing a live musical performance via Zoom, use the strongest wifi available, leave the "automatically adjust microphone volume" box unchecked so that the software doesn't attempt to auto-adjust sound levels based on the preset for speaking voices, and make sure everyone else is on mute. At time of writing, Zoom has a live performance audio option in Beta; video chat technologies are beginning to accommodate multiple instruments and voices in different environments. Encourage participants to lower their bandwidth or data usage by turning off their HD video and for people to only share their screens for as long as necessary.

No solution is perfect. Software is ever-changing. It is important to consider cost, encryption, security, simplicity of the user interface, number of users allowed, and the ability to record.

Live Streaming

You can choose to livestream an event that is happening in-person with many people physically present or you can livestream a single speaker or a group call. Popular livestream platforms include YouTube (owned by Google), Facebook Live, Twitch (owned by Amazon), and Instagram Stories (owned by Meta). The benefit with these platforms is that all you need is a smartphone (or computer) and a free account. Most of these platforms also include a space where audiences can ask questions or post comments in real time. Platforms like YouTube also make it easy to save the video so that it is available after the event ends so that people can watch the event at a later time, making the event even more accessible. YouTube also auto-generates closed captioning for videos.

Choosing a Hybrid Conference Format

When done well, hybrid conferences enable people to gather in-person while creating the opportunity for others to participate from afar. When done poorly, in-person and virtual participants all leave the event feeling dissatisfied. Hybrid conferences require the most advanced preparation and ongoing moderation of the three options.

Hybrid conferences are most successful when organizers allocate sufficient staffing for the virtual rooms and virtual participants. More information (including a step-by-step set up) is available in the tech section on page 55, but plan to have one person in charge of monitoring the virtual livestream and comments per workshop, panel, roundtable, or talk. Having dedicated crew members who can respond to technical difficulties and guide presenters and participants ensures a smoother experience for everyone involved. Proper staffing means that care for all participants can be centered, whether folks are in-person or virtual.

Colonial Context of Space and Land Acknowledgements

Acknowledging the history of unceded territories on which your conference is taking place, as well as the history of the space, is an important practice. Land or territory acknowledgements occur at the beginning of public events. They are often concise and follow a format of: "I want to acknowledge that we are on the traditional territory of [nation names]," though they can be more comprehensive. It is important that if you are giving the acknowledgement, you know how to properly pronounce the name of the nation or community. It is even better if you can learn the name of the nation or community in its original language. Ideally a member of that community will give the opening address. You need to financially compensate this person and provide an honorarium gift.

The violence of the colonization of North America is not relegated to the past. The ongoing impacts of colonization shape our present society. Land acknowledgements raise awareness about Indigenous presence and land rights. They encourage settlers to recognize the history and political reality of the United States and Canada, which is often omitted from school curriculum.

Native Land Digital (Native-land.ca) has created an invaluable resource, including a map that indicates Indigenous territories, languages, and treaties, a teacher's guide, and a list of further resources to help people understand the histories of the lands that we live and work on.

Even if your event is virtual only, everything we do is tied to the land. We must always be mindful of the lands that the servers enabling our virtual events are on. Indigenous communities are disproportionately impacted by the mining practices used for the materials that are used to build our computers and digital infrastructure.

There is some critique that land acknowledgements are token gestures, especially when the people doing them and the audience hearing them do not think about the steps beyond acknowledging the territory where the event is taking place. How can we have reconciliation if we don't have justice? In response, Chelsea Vowel, a Métis writer and scholar from the Plains Cree speaking community of Lac Ste. Anne, Alberta, writes: "If we think of territorial acknowledgments as sites of potential disruption, they can be transformative acts that to some extent undo Indigenous erasure. I believe this is true as long as these acknowledgments discomfit both those speaking and hearing the words. The fact of Indigenous presence should force non-Indigenous peoples to confront their own place on these lands."[1]

Land acknowledgements are merely a starting place. They do not replace the necessary work of reconciliation. The Truth and Reconciliation Commission of Canada's 94 calls to action (trc.ca/assets/pdf/Calls_to_Action_English2.pdf) provide a framework for this work.

Acknowledging Other Forms of Violence Related to the Space of the Event

The United States and Canada built their nations through the practice of enslaving African and Indigenous peoples. The violent legacy of slavery continues across society ranging from racialized economic disparity, high rates of incarceration of people of color, and lower life expectancies and less access to medical care for communities of color. I hold many events and conferences at McGill University. The founder of McGill University, James McGill, was a slave owner and he economically benefited through his choice to enslave others. With this money, McGill University came into existence. I acknowledge this fact at the start of events I host on campus as the histories of violence within our institutions continue to influence and impact the kinds of conversations that are had. I encourage you to think critically about the role of space in the conferences that you organize.

TIMING

Will your conference be synchronous, asynchronous, or synchronous with recordings?

Synchronous

A synchronous conference is ephemeral. People either go to an event or miss it. Benefits include people feeling motivated to go to the event knowing it will be their only opportunity. Presenters might feel more inclined to experiment with ideas or be spontaneous. Synchronous-only events do limit who can participate.

Asynchronous

An asynchronous conference can take many forms. Presenters might pre-record presentations and share them on a conference website. Alternative

[1] Beyond Territorial Acknowledgements https://apihtawikosisan.com/2016/09/beyond-territorial-acknowledgments/

asynchronous conferences might consist of collecting and distributing materials such as zines to all participants. The first asynchronous conference I ever attended was Climate Change: A View from the Humanities, held in 2016. The organizers sought to create a close-to-carbon-neutral conference by discouraging travel. Participants pre-recorded video presentations and attendees asked questions in a comment section. While some participants were able to make connections, the experience served as a reminder that even if components of the conference are asynchronous, it can be useful to include synchronous events where participants are encouraged to interact.

Asynchronous conferences can be useful forums for knowledge sharing, but unless they include some synchronous components such as in-person, virtual, or hybrid social hours, these events are less useful for networking, community building, and socializing. Furthermore, as participants might know that they can access materials at any time, they might actually continue to procrastinate interacting with video recordings or printed documents. If you do organize an asynchronous conference, consider having a chat function or a way that participants can ask presenters questions. Platforms that facilitate virtual interactions such as Gather Town might be useful for your conference.

To Record or Not Record?

Many folks love the idea of recording events. On the one hand, recordings can (1) make materials accessible to a larger range of folks after the conference has ended, (2) serve as an important record of what occurred during the event, and (3) enable participants to attend panels or other conference events that were scheduled concurrently. However, recordings can add another layer of complexity. While many webinar and online meeting platforms enable recordings to either the cloud or desktop with a click of a button, there are other technical challenges. You will need to determine where these recordings will be stored. Who will be allowed to access the recordings? How will they have access? Will you upload everything to a video sharing platform such as YouTube or Vimeo? Who will transfer the videos to that platform? How will you receive consent from the presenters for the video recordings? Will you provide a form presenters must fill out? What about the participants—especially in participatory events such as workshops in which many folks might appear in the recording? Will you have a blanket statement that by participating in the event a person is consenting to be recorded? How long will the recordings be made available? After that period of availability ends, will the recordings be stored anywhere or deleted?

Furthermore, people might feel more guarded and less willing to experiment with ideas knowing they are recorded. If you have included CART captioners or language interpreters as part of your event, fees are often higher if the event is recorded, so you will need to adjust your budget to account for the recording fee. Participants might be less likely to participate in events synchronously if they think they will watch the recording later (which they may or may not do), and this can impact the discussion and participation during the synchronous event.

Technical Tips

The sound quality will be improved if the speakers use a microphone.

If you do decide to record your conference events and have hired CART captioners, you will want that set of captions included in the video rather than the auto-generated captions from services such as YouTube. The following instructions are specific to Zoom but will be similar on other platforms. After the conference event ends (either a single event or maybe you have had the same Zoom meeting going for 8 hours), you will need to download the recording and the transcripts if prompted to do so. Download the recording package from the Zoom website once Zoom has finished processing the recording. You will need to clean the CART generated transcript.

I am grateful to Kit Chokly for creating a template for cleaning the transcript so it is useful on video services such YouTube. Thanks Kit for giving us permission to share!

Template for Cleaning the Transcript

- Create a new Google Doc and copy/paste in the contents of the .vtt captions file
- Title the doc "[EVENT or PRESENTER NAME] Transcript"
- Go Edit > Find & Replace
- Ensure the that "Use regular expressions" box is checked
- Follow the following instructions, copying and pasting the content (including any leading or trailing spaces) within the quotes.

NOTE: *If something weird happens in this process, you can always go Edit > Undo and try again.*

» Find: "[0-9][0-9]:"
» Click: "Replace all"

Repeat:

» Find: "[0-9][0-9].[0-9][0-9][0-9]"
» Click: "Replace all"

Repeat:
» Find: " –> \n   >>"
» Replace: ">>"
» Click: "Replace all"

NOTE: *If this doesn't work, try replacing ">>" with "»" in both fields and adjusting the number of spaces before it in the Find field.*

Repeat:
» Find: "\n\n –>"
» Click: "Replace all"

NOTE: *Make sure the previous content in the "Replace" field is deleted. You may again need to play with the number of line breaks ("\n") or spaces in the Find field.*

Repeat:
» Find: " "
» Replace: " "
» Click: "Replace all"
» Click: "Replace all" again

- You should now have a relatively clean transcript. If it doesn't look perfect, that's okay!

You can now use this cleaned transcript instead of the auto generated captions.

SCHEDULING

You will never schedule your conference at a time that will be ideal for everyone. People have a variety of work schedules, caregiving responsibilities, travel plans, religious holidays, and their own preferences. Timing of the event greatly influences how inclusive your event will be. Your target audience will be key in making this decision. If it is midday, people might not be able to leave their 9:00-5:00 office job to attend. If it is after 9:00-5:00 work hours, parents or people who have caregiving responsibilities might not be able to attend. Facilities might not be free or available on weekends. Friday nights can prevent observant Jewish attendees from coming and Sunday mornings could prevent various Christian attendees. There will never be a perfect time for the event, but think about the group you are hoping to target. There are some factors you definitely want to consider:

- Do the dates conflict with another conference or major event for my field or the target group of conference participants?

- Would the event happen during an important festival or holiday in the location of the conference and thus drive up the cost of hotel rooms and travel tickets?
- Do certain dates drive up venue costs?

FORMAT OF INCLUDED EVENTS

Conferences consist of a variety of events. While every conference is unique, there are a few event formats that are common within conferences. Of course, be creative and make your conference your own!

Welcoming Remarks

Oftentimes conference organizers welcome participants with some welcoming remarks. These statements often include a mix of practical updates to the conference program, a series of thank-yous to collaborators, sponsors, grants, and other folks and institutions that made the conference possible, land acknowledgements, and some words about what the organizers hope participants take away from the conference. These remarks are sometimes followed by a keynote lecture; if this is the case, the organizers often then read the bio of the keynote lecturer at the end of their remarks.

Keynote Lectures

Keynote lectures are typically around 45 minutes long, followed by a Q and A period. Some conferences have a keynote talk on the night before the conference begins or on the first morning of the conference. Typically keynotes are meant to set the tone for the event and bring all conference participants together. Oftentimes a leader in the field is invited to give the keynote address. It is typical for keynote speakers to be paid an honorarium ranging from hundreds of dollars to more than 2000 dollars. You might decide to have a group keynote, with several speakers, although this format is quite rare. You might decide to forgo a keynote, instead emphasizing the various forms of knowledge all participants bring to the conference.

Panels

Panels often consist of 3 to 4 participants sharing papers or presentations for typically around 15 minutes, each about a related topic. There is sometimes a panel chair who reads the presenters' bios and keeps track of the time. A Q and A period often follows the presentations. Panelists might share slideshows or other visual components. It is typical for panel events to last around 90 minutes, including the Q and A.

Roundtables
Roundtables typically consist of 3 to 5 participants chatting about a single topic. Rather than each participant sharing individual papers, projects, or presentations, usually a chair or panel lead has prepared a series of questions for the group to discuss, before opening up the discussion to audience Q and A.

Workshops
Workshops can take many forms. My preference is that workshops have an interactive component. The speaker or speakers share practical experience and then have activities for participants to try. For example, a podcast workshop might have participants experiment by making a short 2 to 3 minute podcast episode, practice cutting together audio on an open source audio editing platform such as Audacity, and coming together and sharing what they have made at the end of the workshop. Sometimes a workshop ends up looking more like a lecture. Depending on the topic and material workshops can range from 1 hour to 5 hours (or more).

Poster Sessions
Some conferences have presenters share their work on posters that they then stand next to during a specific time period. Other participants can walk up to the presenters and ask them about their posters and work. These sessions can be useful for networking and for people to receive feedback about works in progress.

Performances
Performances at conferences can range from theater, to dance, to music! Depending on what type of conference you are organizing, there might be many or no performances.

Exhibitor Halls
While some conferences have vendors, some conferences also have exhibition halls where participants can sit at tables and share or sell their work. Conventions often have exhibitor halls.

Meetings
Perhaps there is a committee, subcommittee, affinity group, or other group that only has the chance to gather together at your conference. It is common for these groups to set up meeting times to talk about ongoing business, create game plans for the future, and socialize.

Tours and Field Trips
Some conferences organize walking tours or field trips to offsite locations, with tie-ins to the conference theme. Some of these events might be organized by community partners.

Coffee Hours
Depending on the location of the conference, participants may not have other food options. Either organized by the conference, by community partners, or by sponsors, coffee hours can be spaces for people to network or socialize over coffee, tea, and light snacks.

Meal Times
Less traditional, but always key to conferences I organize are meal times. While some conferences might provide food to participants, I like to integrate eating into the conference programming. I like to invite the caterers to speak about why and how they create their food and how that speaks to the conference theme. For the Food, Feminism, and Technology conference, my co-organizer Alanna Thain had the idea to have everyone drink their coffee together, with guided tasting, as the founder of the roastery and Dispatch Cafe Chrissy Durcak talked to us about her company's approach to coffee. Throughout the conference, artist and chef Lisa Myers was cooking in the same room as conference workshops, panels, and roundtables, making the labor of the food preparation visible. Lisa then guided participants through our meal and as we ate, she explained her artistic practice and performed artwork about colonialism, blueberries, and residential schools. At the Oxford Food Symposium, participants eat all of their meals together and each day's opening remarks are followed by a presentation by the day's chefs explaining the significance of what we will be eating throughout the day. See the section on the role of food and alcohol on pages 61 to read more about how you can attend to different dietary restrictions, allergens, and more!

Parties and Celebrations
Conferences can include lots of kinds of parties and celebrations. People might celebrate a book launch with a wine and cheese event. Journals or publishers might host a time to mingle. The conference organizers might organize a dance at the conference venue or work with community partners to have after hours gatherings. Wherever these gatherings take place, make sure to include information about transportation, allergens, the presence of alcohol and/or other substances, and other accessibility information.

Other Factors to Consider at Conference Events
Checking Pronunciation
Before the event, encourage anyone making introductions for presenters to check how people pronounce their names and their pronouns before introducing them to the stage. Even if someone's name seems obvious, I still double check pronunciation. Practice the pronunciation of the nations mentioned in your land acknowledgement. Make sure you have the right acronyms and organization names, especially of your sponsors or co-collaborators.

Interpreters and Captioning

Interpreters work with spoken (or signed) words, conveying a message from one language to another (including sign languages). Translation deals with written texts. Your event may require interpreters and translators.

I live in Montréal, Canada. Québec is a francophone province and many of our events are bilingual (French and English). I grew up in Southern California where many events included English and Spanish programming. It's important to consider that, even when the event has materials and presentations in the most commonly spoken languages, speakers from other language groups can be left out.

Deaf and hard of hearing participants may require an interpreter. The location of your event and your target audience will determine your interpretation and translation needs. Make sure that sign language interpreters on a stage are well lit so that audience members are able to see them.

There are international, national, and more local resources for finding interpreters and translators. Internationally, the International Association of Conference Interpreters provides a great tool to find certified professionals (Aiic.net). In Canada, the Canadian Translators, Terminologists and Interpreters Council provides a database for certified professionals outside of Québec (Cttic.org/chercher.asp). Within Québec, see Ottiaq.org. If you are looking for a translator in the United States, you can also use the American Translators Association (Atanet.org).

Human CART captioners can provide live captioning. Canadian Hearing Services (Chs.ca/) is a reliable CART service. While auto-captioning tools do not replace real-time interpretation, these tools can assist in making events more accessible. Powerpoint and Google slides offer auto-transcription tools. Microsoft offers an automated translation plug-in which functions as an auto-captioning device when translating from the presenter's language to the same language, such as English to English. This tool also provides a short url where participants can select their preferred language to follow along on their own devices.

Question and Answer Periods

After lectures, panels, roundtables, and workshops, audience question and answer periods are common practice. During these Q and A periods, there is a tendency for people with more privilege to raise their hands first and dominate the microphone. It can be useful to remind people to be aware of the space that they are occupying in the room. If, as an organizer, you are the one choosing who is asking questions, think about the demographics of the people who are asking most of the questions.

By providing a short pause of 2 minutes between the performance/talk and the Q and A period, people will have time to gather their thoughts and reflect upon their questions before asking them. If there is a panel chair, the chair will likely start the question period with one of their own in order to ease the audience into the Q and A period.

If you have a microphone, please either ask audience members to ask their questions into the microphone or pass a microphone to the question speaker in order that people who are hard of hearing can hear. If there is no microphone for audience questions, please ask that the person answering the question repeat the question before answering it.

If you are worried about encountering the dreaded "more of a comment than a question," no questions from shy audience members, or the possibility of trolling and/or harassment at the event, it is possible to collect audience questions in advance or pass a hat to collect questions. This method also serves as a way you can filter some of the questions if there is a risk of hostile participants. If your event is happening in a digital space, it is possible to filter questions similarly by asking people to send their questions in advance or through an online platform.

A Q and A period can be wonderful for audience members to connect with the speaker. However, it is important to set a timeframe. Many of us have encountered a Q and A period that seems to go on and on and on. This can be hard on an audience and on the speaker. Check in advance with your speaker if perhaps questions can continue in a more informal way after the event.

FORMAT/FLOW OF THE CONFERENCE

Conferences often mix and match a variety of events, including roundtables, workshops, panels, keynotes, meetings, poster sessions, exhibitor halls, celebrations, and more. You may decide to have multiple streams of events happening simultaneously, which means participants will have options about what events they want to attend. You might decide to have a single stream conference where only one event is happening at a time.

Decide if you will use what I will call a "block stream schedule." Within the block stream schedule, regardless of the format of event, each event is allocated 90 minutes.

Do not rush the break periods, as they are pivotal for people to find the room for their next event, use the washroom, and socialize. This period is useful for the presenters during the next block to set up their tech.

The lunch break period will depend on how close your conference venue is to food options if you are not providing lunch. It is useful to provide participants with a map or list of nearby food options.

Below is a simple block schedule that can include an unlimited number of streams. You might also add events that are outside of this block schedule such as tours, celebrations, exhibitor halls, and poster sessions. However, I find starting with this basic schedule to be a useful starting point.

Day 1 Block Schedule Template

- 8:45-9:15 AM: Welcoming remarks by conference organizers and breakfast (including a talk by the caterer if that makes sense for your event). (Some conferences might have a 90-minute block here so that there can also be a keynote.)

- 9:15-9:30 AM: Break

- 9:30-11:00 AM: Block 1 (During this 90-minute period, there will be either a single event, if you are having a single stream conference, or multiple events)

- 11:00-11:15 AM: Break

- 11:15 AM-12:45 PM: Block 2

- 12:45-1:45 PM: Lunch Break

- 1:45-3:15 PM: Block 3 (Encourage presenters for Block 3 to arrive to their rooms 15 minutes early to set up their tech.)

- 3:15-3:30 PM: Break

- 3:30-5:00 PM: Block 4

- After 5:00 PM, you might have parties, celebrations, or collaborative events with community partners.

You might start some mornings later and might end the conference earlier on the last day. Format is up to you and the kinds of events you want to include. Be creative in your planning but make sure to provide participants with a clear schedule so that they can readily locate the events they want to attend.

COLLABORATIVE EVENTS

Collaborative events with community partners can be a useful way to expand your programing without overextending yourself as an organizer. These events can also encourage conference participants to explore other parts of the town, city, or area where the conference is located.

As a conference organizer, I am prepared to schedule events from 9:00-5:00, but I like to collaborate with a community partner to organize mixers, tours, and other events outside of the conference hours. For the Queer Food Conference, we partnered with a local queer and feminist wine bar, Rebel Rebel and Wild Child of Somerville, to have a wine and cheese event at their location. This event encouraged participants to explore more of the Greater Boston Area. The next night, we worked with Big Queer Food Fest to host their event after our conference wrapped up. Maybe you have lunchtime events organized by community partners or pre-conference events that can welcome out-of-town attendees to the city or town.

Perhaps to build hype for your main conference you will host pop up or virtual events in advance of the conference with other related organizations. For example, as part of our lead up to the Queer Food Conference, we co-hosted a virtual panel with the Oxford Food Symposium to highlight the work of queer food folks in Canada, the United States, and the UK.

Collaborative events facilitate networking. Work with your partners to determine ticketing and cost and to discuss whether registration for these events will happen at the same time as the conference registration.

MONEY/COSTS

Is it possible to organize a conference for zero dollars? Kinda. It is likely that money will be involved in conference organizing even if it is in the form of donations. Your decisions around who gets paid, what you pay for, and whether or not you charge for tickets influence the inclusivity of the event.

Funding

You might be asking, how am I supposed to pay for all of this? What if you have to rent a venue, rent audio/visual equipment, and pay performers?

I usually begin planning by imagining I have no budget at all and see what is possible with zero dollars. Then I work from there.

Tickets are one way to fund a conference. Selling tickets, or conference registration fees, in advance can help you have a better sense of your budget and in the case of conferences, make sure that you aren't exceeding the capacity of your venue. Since some folks likely will not show up at the last minute or not attend every event at the conference, you can sell a few tickets over your capacity limit (around 5 to 8% over); however, you want to stick close to the venue capacity. There are numerous online platforms that can facilitate registration and ticketing, such as Eventbrite. However, many platforms take a cut of the sale. Read the fine print.

Selling tickets at the door is a low-tech way to handle sales, but not everyone carries cash, so you might need PayPal or a similar app to accept door registrations. Tickets can also create barriers to access. One solution is Pay What You Can (PWYC) or "Nobody Turned Away for Lack of Funds." Sliding scales can be useful, or consider tiered ticket prices, such as having a policy that students and elders pay a lower ticket price. Another option can be to have scholarships available for some people to attend, as usually the conference registration is not the only cost to participate, especially for people who will need to travel from out of town.

If your conference is a fundraiser, it can be possible to receive donations. Donated space. Donated performances. Volunteer workers. Fundraisers usually still have some form of ticket or collection of a resource: money, cans, and/or labor (such as people coming together to clean the beach or translate documents for community members).

Sponsors can be another option. As an event organizer, you need to decide if you are comfortable taking sponsorships. Likely this will entail that you advertise for the company, which might feel inappropriate depending on your event. Remember that you are in control of what kinds of companies and organizations you take money from. Maybe there is a local business that reflects your values and would sponsor your event? These partnerships can put your audience in connection with local businesses or channel corporate money towards a cause you believe in.

If your conference is associated with an organization, that organization might already have funds that can be allocated towards the conference. Member dues often help subsidize conferences.

Universities and colleges can be a great source of funding for conferences. Even if you are not a student, is it possible to work with a local student group? They often are able to get student activities funding that can pay for speakers, artists, musicians, and performers.

Municipal funding is another great option. It is likely that your town or city has some form of funding available for local events programming. Does your event idea relate to any local community initiatives? Is there a festival, theme, or goal of your municipal government? State, provincial, territorial, and regional funding is a similar option. Many states and provinces offer grants. Consider potential limitations to receiving this type of funding, and how state and municipal control can limit the message or effectiveness of your conference.

National and international grants can be more complex, but depending on your project, can be another option. It is important to note that these kinds of grant applications can require hundreds of pages of paperwork and might not be worth completing for some conferences. Check out what grants you are eligible for a year in advance of your conference.

Foundation and private grants can vary in the kinds of application materials that they require. Money may be available for the kind of work that you are trying to do. Again, I would suggest applying to these kinds of grants after you are already comfortable organizing conferences, as the applications ask about past experience.

Most grants require some form of matching funding. Check if the grant accepts in-kind matching funding. For example, if you plan to hold your event in donated space—with donated sound equipment—and document the show with donated camera equipment, all of that counts as in-kind funding.

A bit of money grows. Funding agencies are more likely to give money and support if they see that you have already gotten some form of funding and support. For my most successful grant application for a speaker and workshop series, which resulted in around a $25,000 grant which required 50% matching funding, I began by getting small contributions of $100. I could then leverage this funding into contributions of $200 and then $500 and then larger contributions. This process is time intensive and required me to write smaller grants to count towards the matching funding. I dedicated 3 months of my life to this work on top of my primary employment. Start small and you can build on this experience.

Paying for Event Programming

As an organizer you will need to make decisions over what kinds of labor you pay for during your conference. It is typical practice that people who have applied to present during workshops, roundtables, and panels are not paid. In fact, usually presenters still pay conference registration fees, as it is common that most participants are also presenters. However, if you invite someone specifically to travel to speak at your conference, it is typical to offer that person an honorarium, such as a keynote speaker. Performers may or may not be paid depending on the context of their performance.

Organizers: Paid or Not Paid?

For the average 2-day conference, I have typically spent around 200 hours organizing the event. I have never been paid for organizing a conference and have volunteered this time. There are some circumstances in which organizers are paid for their labor. Relying on volunteer labor limits who is able to do conference organizing work and can be a class issue. As a conference organizer, I do not charge myself registration fees. If organizers are paid, that also might impact the decisions over whether or not the rest of the conference crew is paid.

YOUR TEAM
Organizers
Are you organizing the conference alone? Are you working with multiple people?

If you are working with other people, I recommend being transparent about expectations and working with a few folks that you trust. Make sure that your task lists are clearly designated. Organize regular check-in meetings and establish a system for communication. Be clear about when tasks will be completed, procedures for finishing tasks if someone has fallen behind, and how you would like to handle disputes during a period when everyone is feeling enthusiastic and happy to be working together. Clear and kind communication can make organizing the conference a much more positive experience.

Staff and Volunteers: Your Conference Crew
No one fully organizes a conference alone. Even if one person is in charge, a conference only exists through the efforts of everyone involved. Depending on the budget of the conference, the conference themes, and the organizers' capacity and network, you might pay people to work at the conference or have people volunteer to work shifts in exchange for free entry to the conference, free meals, a t-shirt or uniform, and/or other forms of compensation for their time.

It is helpful to write out a list of what roles you might benefit by having staffed. While it is tempting as an organizer to think you can handle everything or most things, you will likely need to be handling things on a bigger scale and popping in and out to cover unanticipated challenges or details. It is useful to have folks designated to cover specific tasks so you can rove throughout the conference and allocate resources as needed.

Some typical conference crew/volunteer roles can include, but are not limited to:

Sign-In Table/Check-In
Folks will distribute name tags, conference materials or SWAG bags, point people in the direction of rooms, and be there to answer questions.

Greeters

Folks will help direct people from the front of the building to the sign-in table. If there's a central public transit drop-off point, bike parking lot, or car parking lot, you might want a crew member there to direct people to the sign-in table.

Room Monitors

Folks will help presenters connect to the projector or other technology such as mics, amps/speakers, and the internet (if needed). If you are hosting a hybrid conference, the room monitors will be especially useful. Monitors can ensure panels start and end on time. The busiest period for room monitors is the 15-minute period between events in the room when the monitor must help one set of presenters move out while the next group sets up their tech and/or materials.

    Hybrid conferences require more staffing. To relieve the stress of the video stream dropping, I recommend that every room that is livestreaming and every room with a livestream feed being projected into it has one room monitor. This monitor will make sure that the online and in-person folks are able to hear the audio and see the presenters. The monitor can assist with time keeping and tech set up. Room monitors can also facilitate the question period, either reading questions aloud from virtual participants or sharing in-person questions with online presenters in case the audio quality of the initial question was inefficient. These room monitors are not the same as the IT crew.

Food Set Up

If you are providing food, this crew will make sure that food is arranged, signage identifying items and potential allergens are placed next to the dishes, and plates, bowls, cutlery, and napkins are on the table. If you are working with a caterer, it is useful for the food team to have the caterer's contact number. Ideally schedule food to arrive at least 30 minutes before you serve it so that that food crew can do the set up. This crew will likely also help move the trash, compost, and recycling out of the space after the meal ends (even if you are working with a venue with a cleaning staff).

Facility Check Up

Folks will check that rooms are clean and the bathrooms are properly stocked with toilet paper. This position might be paired with food set up and clean up.

Clean Up Crew
Depending on the kinds of events that your conference includes, you might need to clean up between each event or just at the end of the day. As the conference organizer, while you will be partaking in all roles to various degrees, I think it is important that you always partake in the clean up.

Photographer
As an organizer running around, you might forget to document the event. Establishing one or two folks as the event photographers can ensure documentation of the event. Having photos can serve as useful memories and also can be useful to share with any sponsoring organizations or to share for future conferences and future sponsor and grant applications. It might not be appropriate to photograph certain conferences, so use your best judgment. You might also ask participants to indicate whether they consent to being photographed, as well as sharing where these photos will be used.

Pre-Conference Meeting
While it might not always be possible, I recommend having a meeting with volunteers in advance of the start of the conference. Having this meeting and run-through the day before the conference can allow you to practice using the tech and make sure that everyone is on the same page. After the run-through, I recommend sending every volunteer/crew member an email with reminders of what you covered. This email is useful to share in case anyone had to miss the meeting or forgot any details.

Make sure the crew knows who to contact and how to do so in case any problems arise.

T-Shirts/Uniforms
It is useful to have some way for conference participants to identify the conference crew. A simple technique is to have a conference crew t-shirt, hat, or some other article of clothing that is easily identifiable, often with the name of the conference. Distribute these items in advance of the start of the conference, often at the run-through meeting.

Shifts
I recommend having crew shifts divided into blocks, especially if you are running a block schedule for the conference. For example, if your morning period consists of a welcome period (such as a breakfast with introductory remarks), event # 1 (such as a workshop or panel) for 90 minutes, a 15-minute break/transition period, and event # 2 (such as another workshop, roundtable, or panel) for 90 minutes, you might assign a volunteer to cover the room

monitoring shift from 15 minutes before event # 1 until the end of event # 2. This shift would be 3.5 hours and the volunteer would still be able to see 2 events, while assisting with the tech and time keeping. The rest of the day would be for that volunteer to use as they wish. They would be compensated with a free lunch. The next volunteer covering that room would arrive 15 minutes before the next two blocks (blocks 3 and 4) would begin.

You can communicate with your crew in advance about their availability, accessibility needs, and their interests. If you have someone who is terrified of technology, having them monitor a livestream during a hybrid conference is probably going to just stress everyone out.

Let your volunteers tell you about their accessibility needs. Don't assume. Room set up or assisting the caterers to set up food might not be ideal for a crew member who is unable to lift heavy loads. Mobility disabilities might prevent a volunteer from leading a tour of the venue, but perhaps that volunteer would love to be at the check-in table.

When speaking with your crew about their availability, make sure to ask:

- What hours can they work?
- How long do they want to work? (You might have a minimum number of hours crew members must commit to, but some tasks might be shorter than others. By indicating length of tasks, crew members can also indicate what is possible for their accessibility needs.)
- What are their accessibility needs?
- What are their interests? Are there any tasks they are especially excited about?
- What do they want to avoid, if possible?
- What are their dietary requirements/restrictions/allergies (if you are providing meals for your crew)?
- What are their t-shirt or uniform sizes? And if you have several t-shirt options, what are their preferred designs?

Try to maintain an open line of communication where your crew feels comfortable to ask questions, share concerns, and reach out for support. Asking about accessibility needs early on for all crew members can make participation available for parents, caregivers, people with different disabilities, and people who would like to participate but also have to balance other work responsibilities. We want to make sure that the conference is accessible for participants, but remember that your crew members are also participants. Let us take care of the people who are making the conference possible.

CALL FOR PAPERS/PRESENTATIONS (CFP)

You will need to circulate a Call for Papers/Presentations (CFP). The CFP has a few key pieces of information that you need to communicate.

- Short description of the conference: what is it? (2 to 3 sentences)
- Where is the conference happening?
- When is it happening?
- What kinds of events will be happening (panels, workshops, roundtables, etc.)?
- What kinds of topics are you interested in having discussed at the conference? (1 to 3 sentences)
- I like to share the conference registration cost on the CFP so people will know if they can afford to go/if it feels worth it for them. I am against requiring registration to apply to present as it creates unnecessary barriers and exclusion, though some conferences require membership fees to apply.
- Guidelines for submission (see below)
- Contact information in case people have any questions

Below is a template of submission guidelines that you can adapt for your own needs. This template is based on the CFP for the Queer Food Conference.

Template: Submission Guidelines

Sessions will be 1.5 hours (or whatever length you decide).

Types of Sessions:

Panels *of 3 to 4 papers with a chair/commentator. We strongly encourage the submission of full panels. You do NOT need to include someone to perform the chair and/or comment role as part of your application (but you are welcome to include someone).*

Roundtables, *of 4 to 5 people who present, discuss, and interact with the audience on a single topic, theme, or issue. You do NOT need to include someone to perform the chair and/or comment role (but you are welcome to include someone).*

Workshops *with 1 to 3 leaders that center on an interactive and practical deep-dive into a subject. We will have use of a demonstration kitchen with two stove tops, a sink, a refrigerator, and monitors to project the action. Presenters will be responsible for bringing their own food materials, but we can supply cooking tools, tasting plates, and utensils (or whatever technical information you need to provide).*

We encourage all full panel and roundtable submissions to include a diversity of scholars and practitioners, including people at all levels of career development and from different institutions and identities.

We will also consider **individual paper submissions**, out of which the program committee will assemble a very limited number of panels.

Finally, we will consider all-virtual panels, roundtables, and workshops. If your panel or roundtable is interested in presenting virtually, please indicate that as part of your submission. Please note that there are two different application forms: in-person and virtual.

Please only apply as part of one panel or paper submission. The exception to this rule is for the role of chair or commentator, which may be performed by someone who is also giving a paper or appearing on a roundtable.

All submissions are due by [date].

The program committee will make decisions and send notifications by [date].[2]

Full panels and roundtables should include:
- *Title of panel*
- *Panel abstract (200 words max.)*
- *Title and abstract for each paper (200 words max.)*
- *Biographical statement with contact information for each participant*

Workshops should include:
- *Title of the workshop or cooking demonstration*
- *Workshop or demo abstract (200 words max.)*
- *Abstract for each contribution (200 words max.)*
- *Biographical statement with contact information for each participant*
- *List of cooking tools required*

Single paper submissions should include:
- *Title of paper*
- *Paper abstract (200 words max.)*
- *Biographical statement with contact information*

Questions should be addressed to the [conference organizers' names] at [conference email address].

---

2 It is useful to tell people a date to expect decisions by to reduce the number of emails you receive asking you when folks will hear back. Overestimate the amount of time it will take.

PRESENTER APPLICATIONS

You will need to have a system for collecting applications for presenters. Even if you intend to accept every application, having applications can help you design the schedule, help speakers prepare materials in advance, and provide you with important information such as contact information, accessibility needs, and more.

You might decide to have several application forms divided by the kinds of events or a single application form with multiple options.

Questions to Ask

☐ Name(s) of presenter(s):

☐ Pronouns of presenter(s), if they wish to share:

☐ Email address(es) of presenter(s):

☐ Other contact information you might require:

☐ Name of paper/workshop/or roundtable: *(NOTE: If the application is for a full panel, make sure to also ask for the name of each individual paper/presentation within that panel).*

☐ Abstract/description of paper/event: *(NOTE: Provide a word count—I recommend 100 to 175 words.)*

☐ If you are organizing a hybrid conference, is this presentation for in-person or virtual attendance? Or is the potential presenter open to either option?

☐ If you are allowing open format events of different lengths, have the potential presenter explain the event and provide a justification for the length of the event.

☐ Technological needs? Projector? Sound/speakers? Other?

☐ Presenter(s) bio(s): *(NOTE: These can be shared later with the panel chair when the chair introduces the panel at the conference. Provide a word count. I recommend 50 to 125 words per person. If the person is applying with a full panel or workshop, you should provide a space for each speaker bio.)*

☐ Accessibility needs: *(EXAMPLES: If the presenter cannot use stairs and half of the venue's rooms are upstairs, make sure to schedule their event in a room where stairs are not a barrier. If the speaker is only able to present if childcare is made available, how can you accommodate this need?)*

☐ If a hybrid conference, a question about how the presenter intends to involve in-person and online people equally *(EXAMPLE: if they are distributing printed worksheets in-person, do they have a link they can share with online participants?)*

Optional information to collect:

☐ Affiliation *(such as organization, institution, university, etc. You might need this information for certain grant agencies)*

☐ A space for the applicant to share anything else they might need to share *(such as a scheduling conflict)*

I recommend using software such as Google Forms, which will help you collect this information in an organized manner. Having people email you this information might mean that you miss submissions in a spam box.

A System for Determining Who Is Accepted

You might receive more applications than your conference can accommodate. It is useful to devise a system for choosing who to accept and reject ahead of releasing the CFP. Whether you are deciding alone or with a committee, write out your consideration factors in advance.

- Is it important to have a diversity of topics?
- Is it important to have a diversity of presenters with different identities (race, class, gender, sexual orientation, disability, age, etc)?
- Is it important to have a diversity of different career levels (early career, students, experts, industry leaders, etc)?
- Is it important to have a diversity of experiences (mixing scholars, journalists, people in industry, artists, activists)?
- Will you prioritize already formed panels (if people can submit a whole panel) or individual papers?
- If someone applies for both the in-person or virtual stream, how will you decide which stream to accept that person for?
- Will you create a waitlist in case any accepted presenters decline the offer?
- Will you offer poster sessions as an alternative?
- What counts as a good application? Detail? Topic? Something else?
- Will you suggest people team up if they have a similar topic?

I recommend having your conference committee use a color-coding system of green (yes), yellow (maybe), and red (no/reject). Have the committee rank the applications. Discuss the greens, yellows, and reds separately. Make sure that you have also met your mandate for the factors you want to prioritize in acceptances.

Try making a sample schedule based on the acceptances to see how many people you can ultimately accept. If there are too many excellent proposals based on your plans, you might at this time decide to add an additional stream. Remember that there will be material constraints based on the physical space of the venue or the capabilities of your video chat/webinar platform for virtual or hybrid conferences.

You also need to decide if you are going to accept more people than you have places for, just the number of people you have places for, or waitlist people. The larger the conference, the more likely some people will reject their acceptance.

COMMUNICATION WITH PRESENTERS BEFORE THE CONFERENCE

There will be several times you will need to communicate with presenters before the start of the conference. The first time is when you inform applicants about the status of their applications (see the below templates). You will also likely need to follow up with the accepted presenters to remind them to register and confirm their participation. Anticipate that at least one person's acceptance or rejection email will end up in their spam box.

Template for Presenter Acceptance

Congratulations! Your proposal _____ has been accepted for the _____ Conference taking place in _____ from _____ [date]. To confirm your participation in the conference, we ask that you register for the conference by _____ [date and time].

We plan to release the conference schedule _____ [date] and at that time open up registration beyond accepted presenters.

Registration for the conference is $_____ [cost]. This registration fee covers (1) entrance to the conference, 2) a curated breakfast by local queer food businesses (with coffee and tea) on both Saturday and Sunday, and (3) _____ [whatever SWAG].

Please register here: [link]

[Then if you have other information to communicate, add it here.]

We look forward to seeing you in _____ [space of the conference]!

Thanks!

The _____ Conference Organizing Committee

Template for Presenter Rejection

Thank you for your proposal to the _____ Conference. We received many proposals and unfortunately we are unable to accept your proposal.

However, there are still ways that you can participate in the conference. In _____ [date] we will be opening up registration for the conference. We understand if you are not able to attend, but we hope we see you at the conference.

Thank you,

The _____ Conference Organizing Committee

Ongoing Communication with Presenters

You will also likely need to update presenters with technical details after confirming participation and before the conference. Presenters will want to know if there will be the possibility to project slides and play sound, as well as the length of presentations. While you want to give presenters plenty of time to prepare for the conference, it is especially important to remind presenters of technical details a week before the conference.

Email Template to Share with Presenters the Week Before (and Again the Day Before) the Conference

The below template is for a hybrid conference. This email can be useful for communicating important technical details. For a virtual-only or in-person-only event, you can still use this template; just remove the technical details that do not apply to your conference.

Dear presenters,

We look forward to your presentations during the _____ Conference.

The following email is long but it contains important information for the conference.

1. *On the schedule [provide a link], you will notice that there is a 15-minute break between panels/workshops/roundtables. Presenters, aim to arrive at your room (whether it is the physical room for in-person presenters OR the zoom room for virtual presenters) at the start of the 15 minutes before your panel/workshop/roundtable starts. Doing so will enable your panel to connect to the room's tech/get set up for the livestream.*

2. *Every room will have a room monitor/tech monitor. This monitor will make sure that (a) your panel/workshop/roundtable is connected to the livestream, (b) questions from virtual participants will be asked of in-person presenters AND questions from in-person participants will be asked of virtual presenters, and (c) the panel/work-*

shop/roundtable ends on time. The monitor in the physical rooms will have a sign to indicate that the event needs to wrap up in 2 minutes. This monitor will be wearing a black shirt with the conference logo in purple font.

    a. For virtual presenters, your livestream will be projected into a physical room at the conference.

    b. For physical presenters, your livestream will be available for the virtual participants to watch.

    c. We will not record the presentations.

    d. We will distribute the zoom links shortly before the start of the conference.

3. Each panel/workshop/roundtable is allocated 90 minutes. It is important to stay within the time limits of your event so that the next group of presenters can get set up.

    a. If you have 4 panelists, we recommend that you plan for each panelist to speak for around 15 minutes and the remaining 30 minutes can be used for questions from the audience and discussion. Your panel can decide how you want to divide your time. (Example: If you are 3 panelists, will you each speak for 20 minutes? Or will you have a longer discussion period? If you are 5 panelists, will you each speak for 12 minutes or each speak for 15 minutes with a shorter discussion period?) We strongly recommend that your panel makes the decision this week so that each panelist can properly prepare.

    b. If you have a roundtable, we recommend that your group decides on a group of questions that you will discuss in advance. You are also welcome to run your roundtable similarly to a panel.

4. There are no official panel/workshop/roundtable chairs. We strongly suggest that your panel/roundtable designates one person to time keep and to read the presenters' names and title of their papers. The names of everyone on your panel and their paper titles are available on the conference schedule.

    a. You all have access to each other's email addresses (in the CC of this email). However, if you have trouble contacting your fellow panelists, please let us know.

    b. There will be a set of physical time cards in the rooms for the time keeper to indicate how many minutes are left for each person's presentation.

5. Powerpoint/Google Slides: You will be able to display slides in the room. Plan to bring your own laptop and/or have a cloud version of your presentation.

It's not required, but we recommend that your entire panel/workshop puts your slides into a SINGLE Google Slides show. By having one slideshow, we do not have to spend time connecting and disconnecting from specific tech.

    a. You can import slides from PowerPoint, Canva, slideO, and other slide makers into a single slideshow so that you can all have the aesthetics that you like.

    b. This step can save a lot of stress during the presentation period as connecting and disconnecting from tech can be frustrating. For virtual presenters, dealing with connecting and disconnecting from a screenshare can be annoying too.

We are so excited to see you!

    The _____ Conference Organizing Team

REGISTRATION

You will need a system for participants to register for the conference. Even if you will allow day-of, walk-in registration, it is helpful to have advanced registration so you can prepare properly and anticipate the materials you will need.

There are a variety of platforms that can collect payment, collect contact information, and enable you to contact participants individually and as a group.

I recommend using a platform, such as Eventbrite, that includes multiple ticketing options. It can be useful to use a platform that facilitates different registration periods for different groups of participants. For example, when you inform presenter applicants about their acceptance, I recommend requiring that they register to confirm their participation in the conference by a certain date. Having these confirmed acceptances means you can confirm your conference schedule and share it on your website when you open up the conference to general registration. You can also offer incentives for early registration by having a lower ticket cost if a participant registers by a certain date.

Hybrid Registration

Make sure that participants register for in-person or online participation. Your in-person event space will likely have a maximum occupancy that will limit the number of in-person participants. Depending on what software you use for virtual participants, you might have no participant limit or a very large number of virtual participants that you can include. On several registration platforms, you can limit the number of available tickets within each stream.

I recommend that you provide everyone who registers for in-person participation also with the links to the virtual conference stream to encourage people to stay home if they are ill. Providing these links to all registered participants enables folks to engage with the conference materials even if some unforeseen event occurs or care responsibilities impede a participant's ability to attend in-person. Letting registered participants know in advance that everyone will get the online links whether they registered for in-person or online participation will also save you from having to answer a deluge of last-minute emails before and during the conference when your attention will need to focus on many other factors all at once.

Workaround Option

You can always have an online registration form and ask people to wire you money via PayPal, Interac, or a similar platform, send checks, or bring cash to the conference. However, while this strategy will help you cut out the middleman and avoid platform fees, you will have to keep track of a lot more details.

Items to Include on the Registration Form

- Name
- Pronouns (especially if you are printing out name tags)
- Email
- Phone number
- Accessibility needs
- Dietary restrictions/allergens
- If hybrid, in-person or virtual presentation?
- If there is a sliding scale for ticket price, which option of ticket the participant needs
- What days does the participant plan to attend?
- If your conference has an on-site housing option, you might be able to have housing options included as part of the ticket options.
- If your conference has collaborative events with community partners with separate ticketing and/or cost, you might be able to have a check box option here
- Optional: Affiliation (if it is useful to know if someone is from a specific institution)
- If not already built into the platform, a link for the participant to pay for a ticket
- Any other information you need to collect

CONFERENCE WEBSITE

I highly recommend creating a conference website. The conference website serves to provide information to participants and potential participants. You can update it regularly with new information. There are a few key pages that should exist as part of your conference website. Below I explain what information is pivotal for each page.

What to Include

About Page

The About page should answer the following questions: Who, What, Where, When, and Why. Let readers know what the conference is. Tell readers where the conference is happening. Is it hybrid? Online only? In-person only? When is the conference happening? Where can people register to participate (link to the page on your website for registration)? Is there a final day to register? You can also include information about the background of the conference and the motivation for creating it.

Call for Papers/Presentations (CFP) Page

This page will have your CFP. Include a link to the submission page or include instructions for how people proposing presentations can submit. After the deadline for submission has passed, consider moving this page to a less prominent part of your website.

Registration Page

Even if you are using an external website for registration, the registration page should explain how participants can register for the conference and what dates registration closes. If participants must pay to attend the conference, you can explain pricing here, especially if there is a sliding scale. If you are providing housing that requires separate registration, indicate that on this page.

Contact Page (with Conference Email)

Have a page with contact information. I recommend setting up a conference email address that you set up to streamline all conference correspondence. You can forward this email address to your main email address to receive alerts, but retain the emails in the conference email account to have a record. Link to any social media accounts affiliated with the conference here.

Schedule Page

Here you can include a copy of the conference schedule. I recommend including a table with the different streams of the conference so participants can see what events are happening at the same time. Consider using color-coding within the table so participants can identify different kinds of events. For example, a blue background might indicate a performance whereas a green background may be a roundtable. Below the table you can also include the abstracts of peoples' presentations and even speaker bios. You may decide to organize these by time slot or alphabetically. If you are printing a conference program, consider linking to a PDF version on this page.

Accessibility Page

Include information about location, bike parking, public transit and bike share programs, and car parking (including fees). Provide information about captioning, interpretation, and if your event is virtual or hybrid, the accessibility features of the online platform. Share information about where all-gender and wheelchair accessible bathrooms are located at the venue. Include the details about childcare, spaces to breast/chest feed, and chill-out spaces. Include information about health resources, such as COVID-19 precautions. (EXAMPLE: Will you have free masks available? Will you require masks to attend?) If you are providing food and/or drinks at the conference, explain what dietary requirements, allergens, and religious requirements are met. Here you can share information about the wifi access. This page can be a place to be transparent about the ticket price and why you have a certain price tag. You can also explain if there are any scholarships available to make participation more accessible.

Local Info Page

If you will have participants traveling to your conference from out of town, it can be useful to share information about other resources in the local area. For example, for the Queer Food Conference I shared information about the Boston public transit system and queer resources and businesses within the city. If you are providing housing options, share this information here (or on its own standalone page). If you are not providing housing, share information about local options. I've also used this page to highlight local queer businesses for when conference participants were looking for spaces to eat, drink, socialize, and shop nearby.

SWAG/Merch Page

If you are providing the option for participants to pre-order or purchase SWAG items such as conference t-shirts, hats, or other materials, you can design a SWAG/Merch page.

Additional Events (Optional)
If your conference has partnered events, especially those with separate ticketing, it can be useful to have a web page sharing information about these events and linking to their registration pages.

Publications
If you are going to make a publication such as an anthology, collaborative zine, or edited collection after the conference, you might consider putting this information on your conference website before or after the conference. Include information about how people can submit their materials.

Anything Else You Need to Share with Your Participants
Add additional pages as necessary!

How to Build It
Even if you don't know how to code, there's a large range of website builders. I recommend, whether you are building your site from scratch or using a website-building company, you buy your own domain name separately so you can change hosts as you need. I build many websites on Blogger and GitHub, avoiding paying hosting fees and just buying a domain name. It is outside of the scope of this zine to explain the step-by-step process of web design; however, even without prior experience, you can do it! You might also solicit the help of a friend with web design.

PUBLICITY AND ADVERTISING

There are several points at which you will need to publicize your conference. You will need to share your call for papers/presentations (CFP). You will need to alert people when registration is open. If your conference is already affiliated with an organization, you might be able to just publicize the event on the organization's website, listserv, and social media. Consider sharing on related listservs and your personal social media. Also encourage other people within your network to share your CFP and information about conference registration. Make use of your already established connections!

I recommend establishing social media accounts for the conference in addition to the conference website. Here you can share graphics and photos before, during, and after the conference. Creating this online presence is especially useful if you plan to have additional iterations of your conference or to release publications based on the conference proceedings.

While you may want to take photos during the event, designate someone on your conference crew to document the conference. Make sure to take a photo with your co-organizer(s), as you might forget as you will constantly be running around during the event. Create an online folder where your conference crew or even other participants can upload their photos.

CONFERENCE AESTHETICS AND DESIGN

While not required, I recommend deciding early on in your planning process what your conference aesthetics are. It can be useful to have visual coherence between the website, forms, and marketing. Even picking a color scheme and a font can bring a lot of coherence to your publicity and communications. I recommend being intentional with your choices as colors and font convey specific vibes to potential conference participants.

Having a design aesthetic can distinguish your posts on social media and help participants identify your materials. Furthermore, having already made these design choices early on can save time later when you are doing design work for the conference.

You can create a logo or a tagline and use this on conference publications, SWAG, merchandise, and the t-shirts of volunteers. Creating a cohesive design template can make the conference appear more organized, whether or not you elect to use a polished aesthetic.

CONFERENCE PROGRAMS/BOOKLETS AND GETTING CREATIVE

Printing a conference program or booklet is not a requirement but can help make the conference more accessible to attendees without a smartphone. Obviously if your conference is virtual, having the schedule available on a website, in an email, or virtual document can suffice. In-person attendees could scan QR codes spread around the venue linking them to the conference schedule. You can also print the schedule and tape it on walls around the venue and put each room's schedule on or next to that room's doors (if doors are open, people might not be able to read the schedule if it is on the door).

Printing a conference program or booklet can serve multiple purposes. It can serve as a practical document, political manifesto and/or a souvenir. Historically conference programs have even led to massive protest, exciting discussions, and can represent the ethos of a conference. As Margaret Galvan discussed in her book *In Visible Archives*, the infamous 1982 Barnard Sex Conference's program was even censored! The program of the conference that is seen as pivotal in the feminist sex wars of the 1980s was more than just a schedule of events but included writings, art, and political commentary.

In advance of the Queer Food Conference, we collected recipes and headnotes with explanations of how participants thought their recipe reflected queer food. We printed *Cook Out! The Queer Food Conference Cookbook*, which served as a conference program and a souvenir cookbook. The first few pages had the schedule, an introduction by my co-organizer and me, and the paper, roundtable, and workshop abstracts. The following pages had the recipes and headnotes from about one-third of our participants. I hired an illustrator, Amélie Ducharme, to design a beautiful cover and do the layout. In-person attendees got a physical copy for free, and we made a PDF version of the cookbook freely available on the conference website.

I encourage you to think creatively! What kind of program would work for your conference? Depending on the quantity of programs you need, you can print quite a few copies at low cost.

TECH/IT
Gear and Audio Visual (AV) Equipment
It is likely that your conference will require some kind of electronic equipment. If people are speaking, microphones can improve sound quality and projections. People giving a presentation might want a screen to project a slideshow. Maybe you will show a film. Perhaps a band or DJ will play. You may choose to film, record, or livestream the event so that people who cannot attend can still access the event. Decisions surrounding AV equipment can either radically expand or decrease accessibility.

Using AV Equipment to Increase Accessibility
If there is a projection, such as a Powerpoint or Prezi presentation, does the font contrast with the background? Is the font large and clear to read? Encourage presenters to orally describe what is on the slides. This technique is beneficial for participants that have reduced vision or are blind. It is also a useful practice if the event is being audio recorded.

Consider asking speakers to submit materials in advance of the event; this measure makes the event more inclusive for individuals who may not be able to view screens. Along with this, making printed copies available (in larger fonts) can be beneficial to participants. For participants who would benefit from having their own copy of the slides, you can encourage presenters to include a QR code or tiny url link directing participants to a copy of the slides so that they can read more closely or mark up and write notes with their own devices.

I strongly recommend that if your conference has panels, roundtables, or workshops with multiple presenters, you require or strongly encourage folks in a session to put all of their slides into the same presentation (Google Slides can be a useful strategy for doing this). If not all in the same presentation, have everyone load their slides onto the same computer. Changing between computers (especially changing between Mac, Linux, and PC computers) can cause projection systems to fritz. By having all the slides in one spot, you can reduce friction and stress from malfunctioning tech.

When playing videos, turn on closed auto-captioning. Or better yet, hire a CART captioner (although often priced at $335 for 2 hours of work, this option may not be financially possible). It is useful to check in with participants about their access needs in advance.

Ask presenters to use microphones and have the audience ask questions into a microphone or ask the presenter to repeat the question into the microphone. Speaking loudly is not the same.

Acoustics are important for those with hearing impairment. Limit unnecessary background noise.

Avoid using flashing or overly bright lights, as this can cause sensory overwhelm.

Check if the facility has a hearing loop (sometimes called an audio induction loop). This is a special type of sound system for use by people who use hearing aids. The hearing loop provides a magnetic, wireless signal that is picked up by the hearing aid.

If the wifi requires a password, print it in the conference program and have the password or log on instructions posted around the venue. Make sure to have this information available at the check-in desk.

How to Acquire or Rent AV Equipment
- First check out what the venue already provides AV for free. The venue may also offer rentals, which may or may not be the best deal but can potentially save time, hassle, and stress.
- If you are affiliated with a university, even if the event is not at a university, you usually have access to an AV room for free or inexpensive rentals. This equipment can range from microphones, video cameras, cameras, and more!
- Check out your local library for resources. Again, libraries have more than books! Many have lending libraries with different kinds of equipment.

- Borrow from friends.
- If none of the above options work or if you need a particular piece of gear, private rental companies exist.

Make sure that you have the batteries or power cords that you need for this equipment with you ahead of the event. If you are hosting your conference outside, you might need a generator.

Having IT Crew on Site

While having a conference crew to help with tech is useful, it can be equally important to have dedicated tech support on site. Does the conference venue already supply tech/IT support? If your conference is at a university, you might be able to work with the on site tech/IT department. If there is no on site tech crew, make sure to work with your volunteers in advance, practicing the tech.

Do a soundcheck and check all necessary technology before each event starts. If a video is embedded in a PowerPoint or similar presentation, have the room monitor work with the presenter to check that it works before their panel, roundtable, or workshop begins. There is still always a risk that the tech will still fail. Have you made a backup plan?

Hybrid Events Require Extra Tech Prep

Hybrid events are some of the most technically challenging conference formats. If you want to provide a good experience for in-person and virtual attendees, you will need to properly staff conference rooms. I highly recommend having room monitors in each physical room for hybrid events. The following instructions are for conferences that have some rooms with in-person presenters and virtual attendees and some virtual presenters whose panel, workshop, or roundtable is being projected into a physical space at the conference.

Make sure room monitors are in the room 15 minutes BEFORE the panel/workshop starts.

Room Monitoring with In-Person Presenters and Virtual Participants

The following tips are also useful if you are having an in-person conference but recording all events by using a virtual meeting or webinar platform rather than having video cameras set up on a tripod in each room.

Have a computer connected to the Zoom meeting (or whichever platform you are using) in the room. In case the Zoom feed disconnects, have a document named "Links" saved on the desktop of each computer with the zoom links in it. The computer login and password should be written on the computer next to its keyboard.

The room monitors will need to assist the presenters getting their slides onto that computer (this way you don't have to have the presenters connected to Zoom on their own computers). Ask that presenters show up 15 minutes before their panel/workshop begins so they can get the tech set up with the presenters.

Since presenters have been instructed to email their slides, create a virtual link, OR bring a USB stick (something I recommend doing), room monitors can help presenters move slides off of their computers. It is also useful to have a USB stick and a USB-C adapter in each room that can assist presenters moving slides off their computers.

It is helpful if room monitors also bring their own computer, tablet, or phone to monitor the chat so that the monitors can ask questions to the in-person presenters from the virtual attendees. It is useful for room monitors to tell virtual attendees that they can ask questions via the chat that the monitors will ask aloud during the Q and A period. Pasting this information into the chat several times during the event can inform virtual participants who join after the opening remarks. If room monitors do not have their own devices, as a conference organizer, make one available for them.

You can require that each panel, roundtable, workshop, or speaker is responsible for their own time keeping. However, since the conference needs to make sure that the panel/Q and A session ends on time so that the next group of presenters can set up, the room monitor can facilitate this process.

Room Monitoring in Room with Virtual Panel Being Projected into the Conference

So that there is more of an interaction between virtual presenters and in-person participants, designate a room that will project the virtual presentations. The room monitor will be responsible for making sure that the livestream is projected into the room.

The room monitors should bring their own computer, tablet, or phone to monitor the chat so that they can ask questions from the in-person attendees and share them with the virtual presenters. It is useful to let the in-person attendees know that you will be doing this. People in the room can also be logged into the Zoom webinar and type their own questions: just make sure that their volume is off so that there is no reverb.

SWAG AND MERCH

*M*aybe you have gone to a conference before and gotten a cheap plastic object with the conference name emblazoned upon it. When I see these kinds of objects at a conference check-in desk, I imagine the object soon breaking and languishing in a landfill long past my own demise.

SWAG (an acronym for Stuff We All Get or Souvenirs, Wearables, and Gifts), however, can be done thoughtfully if tied into the theme of the conference and produced in a way that reflects the conference theme.

Does the SWAG have anything to do with your conference theme? For example, if you are hosting a queer wine producer conference, are you providing a reusable wine glass that participants can use throughout the weekend and beyond?

How was the SWAG produced? Have you relied on exploitative sweatshop-produced materials or are you providing attendees with bags containing snacks or items made by local producers? Are the people making the goods being fairly compensated?

If you want to have t-shirts or other apparel, could you have an opt-in option so that attendees who would love a t-shirt can have the option to have one but that the cost isn't passed on to participants who have no interest in wearing it? Having a link on your website where participants can pre-order merchandise can help you print or build a certain amount of objects in advance without generating waste. If participants are excited about any merch that they saw at the event, consider keeping the link available so folks can continue to buy it.

CONFERENCE INFRASTRUCTURE

*T*hinking intentionally about conference infrastructure can lead to a smoother conference experience for organizers and participants.

Conference Check-In/Sign-In Table

It is important to indicate to conference participants in advance of the conference start where they can sign in, find necessary information, and be welcomed to the conference. If a conference is happening in a single building, having the check-in table near the front entrance can make it easy for people to find. If you are hosting the conference on a large campus, around a city, or on rural lands, make sure that participants have the coordinates of this table so they can navigate to it readily.

The role of the conference check-in/sign-in table is multifold. This table is where participants can announce that they have arrived. They can gather or make their name tags. They can pick up conference materials, such as a conference program, SWAG, meal tickets, or any other materials you need to give them. If your conference includes housing, decide if participants will pick up their room keys here or at another location near the residences. This table also serves as a de facto information table where participants may request directions, share concerns, or ask any other questions.

It is useful to have the most amount of volunteers on the first morning of the conference, if you are having a multi-day conference. However, there should always be one person at the table, as participants might arrive late, only attend part of the conference, or also just want a place where they can find information.

What to have at the table:

- List of participants: Have multiple copies. If your conference is larger than 50 participants and you expect everyone to arrive around the same time to the table, you might divide the list into different sections of the alphabet. For example, A-K last names go in line one to check-in and L-Z in the other line, or something like that. Either way, make sure that the volunteers at the table have multiple copies of the participant list.
- Pens and markers to check names off the list
- Name tags: you can either print name tags in advance or have attendees make their own. I am a fan of having participants write their own names and pronouns.
- Conference programs and conference schedules: Have you printed a program? Give it to folks when they sign in. Even if the schedule is only available for participants on the conference website, it is useful to have a QR code near the check-in table so participants can readily find the schedule. It can also be useful to print out a copy of the schedule and have it near the check-in desk so volunteers can readily answer questions about upcoming events and locations. Having a couple of printed copies can also make the conference more accessible for participants without smartphones.
- Cash box or way to digitally accept payments: If your conference allows walk-ins and has a participation fee, you will need a way to collect money. There are lots of different apps for collecting money via phone. Some participants may want to pay in cash so it is useful to indicate whether or not cash, card, or e-payment will be accepted.

- Volunteer schedule/task list: It is useful to have a copy of the volunteer schedule so volunteers have a place they can quickly check without needing their phone or other device.
- Room keys and SWAG are often distributed at this location.
- Masks for participants to mask are also often distributed here.
- Construction tape (so it doesn't damage wall paint), blank white paper, and markers in case you need to make any last minute signage.
- Lost and found box: Even if you have another lost and found location, it is likely participants will bring and/or search for objects at the check-in table.
- Emergency contact numbers, including facility numbers. Is there a leak and you need to let the venue know? Is someone having a health crisis? Providing volunteers with a plan of who to contact in advance is useful, but having a document with these numbers at the sign-in desk can empower your team to handle a crisis or challenge.

Staging Area/Volunteer Area

Depending on the venue of your conference, you likely will have a room or space where you store materials that need to be used throughout the conference. For example, you might not want every program or swag right at the check-in desk. You might need to store some technological equipment. It also might be a space where your conference crew or volunteers can store their stuff, check the shift schedule, rest, and/or get snacks, drinks, or meals. Having an extra store of pens, pencils, paper, and tape can be useful. A first aid kit, extra toilet paper and sanitary products, and other materials you might need to restock (in case the venue does not already do this for you) are useful to store here too.

Bookseller and/or Vendor Area

If your conference has booksellers or other vendors, it is important to find a location for them where they can get foot traffic, that will also not cause traffic jams in the conference space. Is there a space at your venue that promotes circulation, where participants can flow in and out (maybe with separate entrance and exit doors)?

Try not to put the vendors in the basement (unless the whole conference is also in the basement)! While every venue has its restrictions, hiding the vendors in the basement with no windows, no natural light, and a lack of natural foot traffic can be demoralizing for vendors. You want to make sure that everyone can have a good conference experience.

In advance of the conference, contact your vendors about their needs. Do they need electricity? Will they be bringing their own tables?

If your conference has booksellers and some of the authors are conference participants, is there a way to set up book signings or author talks in the same space where the vendors are so that the books are close at hand? Could you set up some chairs and a microphone in the vendor area or close to it for those kinds of events? Connect the bookseller with these authors so they can try to stock books in advance.

If you have a multi-day conference, is there a way the vendors can store their materials overnight? Packing in and out each day can be time consuming and physically challenging for some vendors. If you have a single vendor or two in a room with a lock, can they store their materials in the locked room overnight?

Washrooms/Bathrooms

If the venue already has all-gender and/or single-use washrooms, include this information on your conference website and map of the site. If the venue does not already have these kinds of washrooms, see if you can add signage to create an all-gender washroom during the duration of your conference.

Are there free tampons and pads available in the washrooms already? If not, put a basket in the washrooms with free menstrual products during the conference.

Will the venue make sure that toilet paper is restocked? If not, make sure to have additional toilet paper to restock bathrooms.

It is also helpful to let attendees know where potable water is available.

Chest Feeding/Breast Feeding Space

Is there a space for people to pump and store milk? If so, make this information available on your website. If the venue does not already provide this space, find a space within your venue.

Chill Out Space

Is there a space where participants can chill out? Conferences can be intellectually stimulating and exciting! They can also be really tiring, emotional, and exhausting. Is there a space at your venue with comfy chairs, quiet spaces, and natural lighting where people can decompress from sensory overload? If not at your venue, can you indicate a chill space in your program where participants may want to visit? While participants are capable of doing their own research, it is often appreciated to know that someone has already indicated some nearby locations.

Networking and Socializing Space
While panels, workshops, keynotes, and performances are exhilarating, conferences are about more than the programmed events. Magic can happen over chance meetings, conversations after a particularly stimulating question and answer period, and even scheduled coffee meet ups. Do you have spaces at your venue where people are encouraged to gather with tables, chairs, and nearby refreshments?

Childcare
While some conferences have the option for children to be involved in programming, it might be necessary to provide childcare as an option in order to make the event accessible to parents and other caregivers. See if your town or city has an organization that subsidizes childcare. You can ask people to RSVP in advance if they require childcare and then as a conference make childcare possible at the event itself. Connecting parents who would like to bring their children to the conference can also make pooling resources more possible.

Amber Berson, Juliana Driever, and their collaborators have created resources and artistic works discussing the exclusion of parents from arts spaces and arts conferences. They emphasize that being engaged with your community (including being at conferences) and being an engaged parent need not be mutually exclusive things. Check out The Let Down Reflex exhibition publication[3] for more! Let's not perpetuate the exclusion of parents and caregivers from conference spaces.

Food and Drink
Does your event involve food? Choices over food and drink can impact the accessibility of your event. Will you be working with caterers? Cooking together?

Food
Will you provide food at the conference? Food can be a lovely way to build community. I like having a conference breakfast provided to participants as part of their registration. I find having breakfast encourages people to arrive for morning events and can serve as an ice breaker.

If you are working with caterers, is there a way to incorporate their labor into the conference itself? If your conference is about food or small business, can you offer the caterers an honorarium to speak from their own experience? While this strategy might not be appropriate for every conference, I appreciate how these kinds of morning events showcase different

---

3 Visit https://www.ProjectSpace-EFANYC.org/the-let-down-reflex for more information.

ways of knowing about a topic and can bring different members of a community together.

Will you be charging for the food? Cost of food can impact accessibility for participation and is a class issue. However, cheap food usually means that the farm workers, the people working in the food processing plants, the people cooking the food, and/or the people selling the food are not paid a living wage. This is a labor issue. This is also a feminist issue as women disproportionately do the kind of underpaid or unpaid work of preparing food. Furthermore this labor is highly racialized and classed and is intertwined with immigration policies that criminalize workers. Cheap food comes at environmental costs under industrialized food systems that disregard biodiversity, use pesticides, and lead to the destruction of ecosystems. It is a difficult balance to make sure that food is priced so that every worker is properly compensated and that all participants can afford the food. There is rampant cruelty, exploitation, and injustice throughout the food chain, even when serving vegan food. Mixing the price of items available can be one way to address these issues.

If you will have a snack table with free treats throughout the day, try to make sure that there is a variety of foods.

When serving food, there are dietary considerations such as vegan, vegetarian, kosher, and halal, as well as common allergens such as nuts, gluten, and soy. If the event involves a caterer, I try to order food that will meet as many dietary considerations as possible at once. Tasty vegan food with a gluten free option tends to accommodate most participants. However, food carries cultural significance. Depending on your conference's objectives, you may make different choices surrounding food.

When participants register for the event, you can add a question on the registration form to ask about any dietary needs.

Drink
Will you be serving alcohol at your conference? The choice to serve alcohol may limit the age of participants for the event. It can also impact who might feel welcome to attend the event. People who wish to stay sober may refrain from attending. I recommend having a variety of events so that people who choose not to drink are also able to participate in some social activities related to the conference.

The choice to serve alcohol may also require a permit. Check far in advance, as liquor permits can be difficult to obtain depending on your venue and city. Many regions also require certification for staff or volunteers to serve alcohol.

Have water available for free and encourage people to bring their reusable water bottles/containers. Restricting access to water can jeopardize the health of people attending the event. Depending on the venue, this may be more difficult due to the infrastructure of the facility.

Serving

- Single-use plastic plates and utensils go straight to the landfill. Is it possible to have food options that do not require utensils? Can you avoid using single-use items? Can you serve food on compostable plates?
- Encourage participants to bring reusable cups and water bottles.
- Have some straws available for participants who may require them to eat or drink.
- Ensure that food is clearly labeled (vegan, gluten-free, kosher, halal, etc) and mark common allergens.
- Have a recycling and compost bin in addition to a trashcan to reduce the environmental impact from the event. Make sure these are well marked. Assign a member of your conference crew to make sure these receptacles are emptied so people have space to properly dispose of their materials.

Housing

If you have people traveling from out of town to attend the conference, they will need a place to stay. Conferences held at universities or within hotels may have rooms available in the facility, sometimes at bulk discounted rates. Some universities make dorm rooms available for conference attendees during the summer or holiday breaks. Some hotels will enable conference organizers to reserve a block of rooms.

It is useful to provide information about housing options available for a range of budgets on your conference website. Some conferences even help connect attendees with local residents who have spare rooms or a couch, though this usually happens less formally due to liability issues that may arise.

WHAT TO HAVE IN YOUR BAG THE DAY-OF

*A*lways have tape, scissors, paper, and a bold marker on you—no matter the kind of conference. Ideally you can have masking tape and duct tape. You never know if you will need to make a sign with arrows to direct people where to go. Masking tape won't rip paint off of walls. Duct tape has a wide variety of applications. Markers, pens, and paper are useful if—shocker—you need to write anything down.

You will want to have clear and visible signs for accessible entrances, parking, washrooms, public phones, transit points, and other conveniences.

Key documents: Carry printouts of the schedule, emergency numbers, your to-do lists, and your volunteer/conference crew work schedule (with their numbers). Have backup copies of the attendee/participant list. Have a map of the venue close at hand to direct lost participants.

Bring chargers, cords, USB sticks, connector cables, a laptop, and phone if you have one! I live in Canada and just from walking to a venue, the winter cold can kill my phone battery. Oftentimes, presenters, performers, and I plan to contact one another by texting before an event. To have a dead phone battery can increase stress unnecessarily. Having backup computer chargers, batteries, extension cords, and USB sticks can be game changers. I often hold events in rooms where I haven't been able to try the tech before. I bring my own computer, connector cables (such as USB to VGA or USB to HDMI), and USB sticks, just in case a computer doesn't work with the tech set up of the venue. Even though you ideally will have done a tech run-through in advance, be prepared and have a backup plan.

To make sure you can attend to any last-minute details as an organizer, it's a good idea to have your phone and laptop with you at all times. Remember, it is likely that people will be emailing you with last-minute questions.

A water bottle and snacks: Make sure to hydrate and attend to your bodily needs. Keep snacks on you!

Making Mistakes

No matter how well you have planned your conference, mistakes and mishaps will happen. Post-conference recaps with your conference crew are key after each day to make sure everyone is on the same page for subsequent days. Give yourself time to reflect on what worked and what didn't (see **Worksheet #2**). Be open to feedback from participants. These moments are growing opportunities that will help you organize subsequent conferences!

WORKSHEETS

The worksheet on the following page will help you brainstorm early in the conference planning process. The second worksheet is to be filled out after each day of the conference.

Feel free to photocopy and re-use these worksheets for your future conferences! If your phone has word detection capabilities, you can turn your camera app on and select the text so you can type your own answers and/or use the email templates more readily.

Worksheet #1: Brainstorming and Key Details

This worksheet is useful to fill out several times. The first time you fill out the worksheet you can write your dreams for the event. You can refill the worksheet once you have the details settled. Update the worksheet in case details change.

General Conference Details

Theme of the conference:

Name of the conference:

Estimated amount of participants:

Estimated amount of speakers/presenters/performers:

Estimated number of events (including workshops, panels, keynotes, or other activities):

Will there be several events happening simultaneously or will the conference have a single-stream (one event per time block) format?

If simultaneous streams, how many?

Length of the conference/how many days?

How many hours per day?

Start time each day?

End time each day?

Dates (may depend on speaker availability and location—but what are your ideal dates?):

Location?

Cost of location to use?

Room capacity within the location?

Other costs associated with the location? (Chair rentals? Table rentals? Cleaning fees?)

Do you need to get a permit to use the location?

Do you need any special licensing? (Liquor permits?)

If you have gone to other conferences, what did you like? How can you incorporate these components into your conference?

If you have gone to other conferences, what did you not like? How can you avoid these issues?

Format of Conference Events

What kinds of events will your conference include?

How long will these events be? If events are different lengths, how will this impact scheduling if you have multiple streams?

Panels?

Workshops?

Roundtables?

Keynotes/lectures?

Performances?

A dance?

A guided tour?

Anything else?

Will you provide honorariums for speakers, workshop leaders, and performers? If so, how much? Cash, checks, e-payment? Who is going to handle the payment paperwork? How long will payment take/what is your payment timeline? Will you pay people before or after the conference? Will you pay in installments?

Partnered Events/Collaborations

Are you organizing every event or will you partner with other folks or organizations to host partner events?

Will partner events happen during the main conference timing or after hours/ outside of conference hours?

Do those events have separate registration or ticketing?

How will you decide which folks to partner with? What values do you want to align with? Are you comfortable with corporate sponsorship?

Funding

What upfront costs do you have? Do you have to make a downpayment on the location? What about website design, domain names, or hosting? Are you paying for any advertising?

What are your estimated total costs, including location, rental of tables, chairs, honorariums for keynote speakers, and tech, catering, or food costs?

Will you apply for grants?

When are the grants due and what do they require?

Will you seek sponsors? How will you decide what kinds of sponsors align with your values?

Will you have tickets? Will they be sold at a sliding scale?

Will the event be free?

Volunteers/Crew

How many folks do you need?

Will people be paid? If not, will they be compensated in other ways (shirts, food, comped conference fees, school credit, something else)?

How long will shifts be?

Will you have a run-through in advance?

How will you communicate with the crew?

Tech Needs

What kind of tech do you need?

Microphones or voice amplifiers?

Speakers?

Cables/extension cords?

Projectors?

Computers? Will presenters bring their own?

Dongles to connect to projectors?

Do participants need a wifi code? Is it publicly available? If not, how will you distribute it?

If there is an artistic installation: what special tech needs do the artists or performers need? How will you collect this information in advance?

Food

Are you going to provide food?

Will you hire caterers?

What types of foods will you offer and how will you make sure to provide food for people with allergies and different kinds of diets (vegetarian, vegan, halal, kosher, etc)?

How will you collect information about the dietary restrictions of participants in advance? Part of the registration form?

Will food be free? Included with certain kinds of tickets? Or available for purchase?

Will you work with vendors such as food trucks and coffee carts? If there is cooking on site, what special tools do the cooks need?

Do caterers need any special equipment?

If there is not running water, how will you make sure to have enough potable water?

Reusable plates, bowls, and cutlery or disposable? Compostable? Will you wash dishware?

Clean Up

Do you have crew members assigned to this task?

Will you have compost and recycling? Is this something already available at the venue or will you have to arrange this yourself? Do you have the bags/supplies necessary?

Worksheet #2: Post-Conference Recap

At the end of the first day of your event, reflect on what went well, what could be improved, and your gameplan for the next day (if you have a multi-day conference). You can also use a version of this worksheet after the conference concludes. It is best to write down reflections when the conference is still fresh in your mind.

What went well today?

What did not go as planned?

What could be improved with the technology/IT?

What could be improved with the conference crew?

Did any crew member have suggestions or complaints?

Did any participants have suggestions or complaints?

Anything else that can be improved?

What will you do differently tomorrow?

Do you need to communicate this new plan with your conference crew?

If so, have you communicated this new plan yet?

CONCLUSION

Dear readers, after reading this guidebook, I hope you are inspired to organize inclusive conferences! I hope you can benefit from the process of my learning from my mistakes.

This handbook would not be possible without the body of feminist and social justice literature that continues to shape me and my work. Thank you to the writers, thinkers, activists, and artists who inspire and challenge me. Thank you to the activists in the disability rights movement who continually bring awareness to the importance of accessibility. Thank you to everyone who has ever attended or supported a conference that I have organized. Thank you for your patience as I learned what worked or didn't work. Thank you to every group and individual with whom I have had the pleasure to collaborate. Thank you to Alanna Thain, Maya Hey, and Megan J. Elias for co-organizing conferences with me. Thank you to Kari Kuo for your edits, Amber Berson for sharing your resources on childcare, and Kit Chokly for sharing your guide to cleaning transcripts.

ABOUT ME

Alex Ketchum, PhD is an Assistant Professor of Gender, Sexuality, Feminist, and Social Justice Studies at McGill University and the Director of the Just Feminist Tech and Scholarship Lab. Ketchum has organized several conferences, including the hybrid Queer Food Conference, the Food, Feminism, and Fermentation Conference, and the food, feminism and technology conference, Circuits de consommation: Art, activisme et la biopolitique du contrôle alimentaire. She organizes a yearly Feminist Research Colloquium and has organized hundreds of events, including lectures, battle of the bands, book readings, organic pumpkin festivals, workshops, and art shows. Notably she has organized over 100 events for her SSHRC funded speaker series: Disrupting Disruptions: the Feminist and Accessible, Publishing, Communications, and Tech Speaker and Workshop Series (see free video recordings of events at disruptingdisruptions.com). Ketchum is the author of several books including *Ingredients for Revolution: A History of American Feminist Restaurants, Cafes, and Coffeehouses* and *Engage in Public Scholarship!* With Microcosm, she has published *How to Start a Feminist Restaurant* (2018) and *How to Organize Inclusive Events* (2020). A historian by training, Ketchum works to make queer and feminist history more accessible. For more information, visit alexketchum.ca.